ENVIRONMENTAL LIABILITY

A Practitioner's Handbook

ENVIRONMENTAL LIABILITY

A Practitioner's Handbook

by

Gordon Campbell
Solicitor

Eversheds, London

CLT PROFESSIONAL PUBLISHING
A DIVISION OF CENTRAL LAW TRAINING LTD

Published by
CLT Professional Publishing
A division of Central Law Training Ltd
Wrens Court
52-54 Victoria Road
Sutton Coldfield
Birmingham B72 1SX

ISBN 1 85811 033 5

Typeset by Dorchester Typesetting Group Ltd, Dorchester, Dorset
Printed in Great Britain by The Lavenham Press

Contents

Preface

Environmental law is a subject which the vast majority of legal practitioners do not deal with on a day-to-day basis. However, most lawyers, other environmental professionals and their clients are aware of the growing risk of environmental claims and potential liabilities. There are few common threads in UK environmental law. We have criminal and clean up penalties contained in a diverse group of statutory regimes and and civil remedies available through traditional common law concepts. Whilst the various statutory provisions are becoming more integrated, each has its own separate history and philosophy. Given the common law's propensity to respond to commercial pressures it is hardly surprising that so much case law is still firmly rooted in the concepts of the industrial revolution. Whilst modern case law is developing very much in fits and starts.

Each of the various regulatory frameworks could easily be the subject of a far larger book than this. However, it is hoped that this work will provide not only most answers for most of the questions raised in the course of general practice, but also a first point of reference for those interested in more complex problems.

Gordon Campbell
Eversheds, London

Table of Cases

Abbreviations

EPA   – Environmental Protection Act 1990
HMIP – Her Majesty's Inspectorate of Pollution
HSA   – Hazardous Substances Authority
HSE   – Health and Safety Executive
IPC   – Integrated Pollution Control
LPA   – Local Planning Authority
NRA   – National Rivers Authority
WIA   – Water Industry Act 1991
WRA   – Water Resources Act 1991

Introduction

History, Context and Future Trends

Contrary to popular belief, environmental law is not a new subject in the UK. For centuries the common law torts of nuisance, negligence, *Rylands and Fletcher* and trespass have been used by injured parties seeking remedies for pollution incidents. In terms of statute law the Environmental Protection Act 1990 is looked upon as a current landmark. However, large sections of this were lifted substantially from the Public Health Act 1875. Local enactments and bye-laws regulating offensive trades can be traced back to the 15th century.

Nevertheless the subject has perhaps received most attention in the last five years or so. One only has to look at the manner in which membership of the UK Environmental Law Association has mushroomed from about 10 people in 1986 to over 1,000 lawyers and other environmental practitioners today.

Before considering the specific environmental liabilities which will be of most interest to lawyers and clients today, it may be helpful to put the current concerns into some sort of historical perspective.

For most of this century environmental legislation has tended to follow the Victorian concerns relating to pollution control, nature conservation and land use planning. Each of these areas has tended to develop separately which is indicative of a fragmentation of environmental administration and control. Each statutory regime has, as a rule, set up its own framework for enforcement, each dealt with by a separate statutory body with very little coordination between these various bodies.

The 1970's saw the commencement of a renewed interest in environmental control, both internationally and domestically. This upsurge in interest was reflected in the Control of Pollution Act 1974. In fact the 1974 Act was not particularly innovative. It introduced important provisions with respect to water pollution, noise control and waste disposal (the first comprehensive set of water controls in this country) but it did not really introduce a comprehensive system of pollution control. For example, there were no provisions dealing with air pollution. The Act continued to reflect the traditional character of UK environmental law. Controls were fragmented between different statutory bodies. Licensing systems backed up by criminal sanctions (or "command and control" systems) were and continue to be the norm.

Historically, environmental legislation has tended to provide a framework for control with very few policy objectives or standards set out. A great deal of discretion is left to enforcement bodies with respect to standards imposed in licences and mode and frequency of enforcement action. The relationship between regulators and industry has tended to be non-confrontational and the public has been, by and large, excluded from consultative processes and not privy to the environmental records held by the various bodies.

As a result the system of pollution control in this country has always tended to be non-legalistic. For example, until recently, there have been few prosecutions or significant civil cases. Many important, and long-standing, parts of our legislation have remained untested in the higher courts.

Modern Framework

Under the Environmental Protection Act 1990 and the Water Resources Act 1991 (formerly the Water Act 1989), a number of important changes are beginning to take place. Although there are still a large number of organisations involved in administering environmental controls there is a move away from local authority control towards larger national (though often regionally based) organisations such as the National Rivers Authority and Her Majesty's Inspectorate of Pollution. This trend will continue with the setting up of the Government's proposed Environment Agency. Command and control systems still prevail but with more detailed legislation and policy guidance. Administrative bodies appear to be more aggressive and exercising their discretion more rigorously. Fines in the lower courts appear to be increasing and there is increased public participation through access to information in registers, rights of private prosecution and rights of consultation. The Environmental Information Regulations 1992 are a clear step in the right direction although implementation is patchy at present.

These changes reflect wide legal and philosophical changes in recent years. In particular, there is now a clear division between the providers of water services (now in the form of private water companies) and the regulation of water standards through the National Rivers Authority. The same philosophy is now being applied to waste regulation. Perhaps more importantly EC policies are requiring a far more rigorous, formal and explicit approach to environmental control than has prevailed in the UK in the past.

Since 1973 the European Community has introduced over 200 pieces of environmental legislation. The European Court of Justice is assuming a more important role. It is developing judicial doctrines on the direct effect of EC measures to national jurisdictions. Individual citizens are being given rights against Member States failing properly to implement EC legislation.

In terms of specific initiatives the Access to Information Directive has resulted in the implementation of the Environmental Information Regulations 1992. The Waste Water Directive and Landfill Directives are also being implemented in UK legislation. The European Eco Management and Auditing System (a voluntary system for monitoring corporate environmental management) and the Eco Labelling Scheme are also emerging.

Looking at recent developments within the EC and current Government philosophy it is likely that there will be increasing reliance upon voluntary instruments aimed at harnessing market forces. Examples include the Eco Labelling Scheme and the Eco Management and Audit System. There is evidence of manufacturers asking suppliers to comply with specific environmental objectives as well as reviewing their own management systems. These trends make it more likely that the courts will be taking a tougher view of what operators should "reasonably foresee" in terms of the environmental consequences of their actions. Whilst such developments will fascinate the academic, should the average commercial practitioner be concerned?

Hitherto, most clients have taken a fairly relaxed view of environmental control which in turn has reflected the non-legalistic approach adopted by the various enforcing authorities. As and when those authorities enforce more vigorously, as has been seen already with the NRA, this approach will change. Similarly the House of Lords decision in the *Cambridge Water* case may give potential litigants the confidence to pursue claims.

In transactional work, purchasers and funders, influenced by US and European developments are asking vendors to supply more information. Solicitors for all parties are being asked to advise upon audit issues and are building professional relationships with their clients' technical advisers. The magnitude of potential claims is such that no lawyer can afford to ignore current issues and future developments. It is hoped that the following text will provide an overview as to the main sources of potential liabilities and assist general practitioners with a starting point for what can be very specialist areas of legislation.

It should be noted that just as environmental problems show scant respect for geographical or ownership boundaries, they also pay little respect to legal "boundaries". A problem relating to air or water pollution may lead to contraventions of several statutory regimes (e.g. statutory nuisance, waste control, Integrated Pollution Control) as well as different tortious liabilities. Readers should resist any temptation to compartmentalise a problem which arises. The enforcing authorities certainly will.

Environmental Information

The foundation for any meaningful advice upon questions of environmental liability must be good quality environmental information. There is no shortage of environmental consultants in the market place willing to carry out surveys, audits and tests. In corporate and property transactions as well as litigation matters, lawyers are learning the benefits of effective team work with scientific professionals.

However, whilst there are definite limits to what the non-scientific lawyer may advise upon, there are many public sources of information which the lawyer can search against and make enquiries of to assist a client.

The traditional culture of British public authorities has not been particularly helpful towards members of the public (even lawyers) making enquiries for information held on their files. However, the Environmental Information Regulations 1992 which came into effect on 31 December 1992 implementing the EC Directive on access to information are aimed at changing this. In summary, any public authority holding environmental information is under an obligation to make that information available to every person who requests it. Whilst specific categories of confidential information are exempted from this obligation the guidance issued by the Department of the Environment makes it clear that there is, in effect, a presumption in favour of release of information. The regulations apply not only to state and local government bodies, but also bodies with public responsibilities for the environment under the control of the state or local authorities (see Reg 2(3)). A recent first instance decision (*R* v *British Coal Corporation, ex p Ibstock* (1994)) confirms that the regulations apply to what remains of our nationalised industries. Furthermore, given the degree of state regulation to which they are subject, there is an argument that the privatised monopolies are emanations of the state and therefore subject to the regulations. This view is supported by the decision of the European Court of Justice in *Foster* v *British Gas plc* (1991) and the unreported first instance decision in *Griffin* v *South West Water Services* (1994).

CHAPTER ONE

Statutory Nuisance

Key Points

- Local Authority under a duty to investigate and duty to act
- Smoke, smell, noise etc must be "prejudicial to health or a nuisance" (common law concepts relevant)
- Notice served on person responsible or owner
- Aggrieved private individuals have a right of action

The statutory regime governing "statutory nuisance" is contained in Part III of the Environmental Protection Act 1990. This replaces and updates the statutory nuisance provisions of the Public Health Act 1936, the Public Health (Recurring Nuisances) Act 1969 and the noise nuisance provisions of the Control of Pollution Act 1974. The fundamental principles remain unchanged. Local Authorities (for these purposes District and London Borough Councils and, in due course, the new Unitary Authorities) are under a duty to inspect their areas from time to time to detect statutory nuisances and to investigate complaints made by residents (section 79(1)). Where an Authority is satisfied that a statutory nuisance exists or is likely to occur or recur it is under a further duty to serve a notice ("an Abatement Notice") requiring:

(a) the abatement of the nuisance or prohibiting or restricting its occurrence or recurrence;

(b) the execution of works and the taking of other steps necessary for those purposes.

Further details of the Abatement Notice procedure are given below.

What is a "Statutory Nuisance"

Section 79(1) of the Act sets out the matters which would constitute a statutory nuisance if "prejudicial to health or a nuisance";

  (a) the state of premises;

  (b) smoke emitted from premises;

  (c) fumes or gases emitted from premises (only applicable to private dwellings);

  (d) any dust, steam, smell or other effluvia arising on industrial, trade or business premises (not including steam emitted from a railway engine);

  (e) any accumulation or deposit;

  (f) any place or manner in which animals are kept;

  (g) noise emitted from premises (except for aircraft noise (apart from model aircraft));

  (h) noise emitted from or caused by a vehicle, machinery or equipment in a street;

  (i) any other matter declared by any enactment to be a statutory nuisance.

Subsections (2)-(12) of section 79 contain a plethora of further exceptions, limitations and caveats relating to this definition. For example, paragraph (b) does not apply to smoke emitted from the chimney of a private dwelling within a smoke control area, dark smoke emitted from the chimney of a building or a chimney serving the furnace of a boiler or industrial plant attached to a building or for the time being fixed to or installed on any land, smoke emitted from a railway locomotive steam engine, or dark smoke emitted otherwise than as mentioned above from industrial or trade premises.

Paragraphs (b) and (g) do not apply in relation to premises occupied on behalf of the Crown, naval, military or air force purposes or occupied by or for the purposes of a "visiting force" under the meaning of the Visiting Forces Act 1952.

With regard to paragraph (g), it is a moot point amongst practitioners as to whether or not the restriction upon aircraft noise applies to the testing of aircraft engines. It is suggested that the exception will only apply where the engine remains attached to the aircraft it serves.

"Prejudicial to Health or a Nuisance"

At first glance, both of these terms have been defined in a deceptively straightforward fashion. Section 79(7) states that "prejudicial to health" means injurious or likely to cause injury to health. With regard to "nuisance", the most frequently quoted dictum is that of Watkins J in *NCB* v *Thorne* (1976):

> "a nuisance coming within the meaning of the [1936 Act] must be either a private or public nuisance as understood by common law".

However these straightforward definitions have been given additional judicial nuances. In *Betts* v *Penge UDC* (1942) Caldecote LCJ held that in determining whether or not an activity was prejudicial to health it was sufficient to show that the premises in question were such as to interfere with personal comfort. In *NCB* v *Thorne*, Watkins J went on to state that:

". . . whatever is complained about must in some way be directed to the health of the person who claims to be or has been affected by the nuisance." A further judicial qualification is now accepted in that to be within the spirit of the Act a statutory nuisance must "produce a threat to health in the sense of a threat of disease, vermin or the like" – Lord Widgery C J (*Coventry City Council* v *Cartwright* (1975)). In that particular case it was held that a deposit of entirely inert materials could not amount to a statutory nuisance. The principle of nuisances having to be within the spirit of the Act has more recently been confirmed in *Wivenhoe Port* v *Colchester Borough Council* (1985).

Additionally, in judging whether or not a given set of circumstances amounts to a statutory nuisance, regard must be had to the character of the neighbourhood in question: "what would be a nuisance in Belgrave Square would not necessarily be so in Bermondsey": Thessiger LJ in *Sturgess* v *Bridgeman* (1879).

Who is Served with the Abatement Notice

The person served with a notice will be the person responsible for the nuisance or where the nuisance arises from a structural defect "the owner" of the premises in question. Where the person responsible cannot be found or the nuisance has not yet occurred, the notice must be served on the owner or occupier (section 80). Special provisions apply with regard to noise in streets (see below).

There is no definition of "owner" in this part of the Act. Two possible interpretations have been advanced for this. Either:

1. Reference should be made to the usual statutory definition of owner (as used elsewhere in the Act) which refers to persons entitled to receive the rack rent whether or their own behalf or as agents or trustees for another (i.e. including people like mortgagees in possession and receivers); or

2. Parliament had the opportunity of inserting such a definition and failed to do so. This was presumably intentional and accordingly "owner" should be given a more restrictive meaning.

The point has yet to be tested in the courts and may be argued either way.

With regard to noisy vehicles, machinery or equipment in streets, if the nuisance has not yet occurred or arises from a vehicle, machinery or equipment which is unattended, the notice must be served on the person responsible for the vehicle etc, or if he cannot be found (or, if the Council so determine) by fixing the notice to the vehicle, machinery or equipment.

Where an Abatement Notice is affixed to a vehicle, machinery or equipment and the person responsible for it can be found and served within an hour of the notice being so affixed a copy of the notice must also be served on that person (section 80A).

The Noise and Statutory Nuisance Act 1993 introduced additional controls in respect of loudspeakers in streets and noisy burglar alarms. In both cases powers are given to Local Authorities who resolve to introduce the provisions of the Act within their areas.

Enforcement

Contravention of or failure to comply with an Abatement Notice is a summary criminal offence, the maximum penalty being a fine not exceeding level 5 on the standard scale or £20,000 for an offence committed on industrial trade or business premises. However, commercial operators will have a defence if they can prove that "best practicable means" were used to prevent or counteract the effect of the nuisance complained of (section 80(7)). The defence is not available in the case of smoke emissions (unless from a chimney) and is not available in respect of fumes or gas emissions. As is usual with statutory defences the onus is upon the defendant to establish the defence. The term "best practicable means" is to be interpreted by reference to the following:

(a) "practicable" means reasonably practicable having regard among other things to local conditions and circumstances, to the current state of technical knowledge and to the financial implications;

(b) the means to be employed include design, installation, maintenance and manner and periods of operation of plant and machinery and the design, construction and maintenance of buildings and structures;

(c) the test is to apply only so far as compatible with any duty imposed by law;

(d) the test is to apply only so far as is compatible with safety and safe working conditions, and with the exigencies of any emergency or unforeseeable circumstances (see section 80(8)).

In cases relating to noise, regard should also be had to codes of practice issued under the previous legislation contained in the Control of Pollution Act 1974.

In the case of *Wivenhoe Port* v *Colchester Borough Council* (1985) it was held that whilst economic factors were relevant, the mere incurring of expenditure, even if it resulted in the unprofitability of a process, was not conclusive.

Private Action

Private individuals aggrieved by the existence of a statutory nuisance may apply to the Magistrates' Court for an abatement order:

● requiring abatement of the nuisance;
● prohibiting its recurrence;
● requiring works to be carried out.

The court can also impose a fine not exceeding level 5 on the standard scale (section 82). Depending on the nature of the nuisance complained of proceedings are commenced against the person responsible for the nuisance or the owner or occupier of the premises in question. The requirements in this respect reflect those relating to service of an abatement notice (see above).

Clean-Up Powers

Where an Abatement Notice has not been complied with the Council may, whether or not they take criminal proceedings, take steps to abate the nuisance and do whatever may be necessary in execution of the notice (section 81(3)). Any expenses reasonably incurred by the Council may be recovered from the person by whose act or default the nuisance was caused. If that person was the owner of the premises, expenses may also be recovered from any person who is for the time being the owner and the court may apportion the expense between persons who caused the nuisance in such manner as the court considers fair and reasonable (section 81(4)).

Where expenses are recoverable from an owner and the Council serves a notice on him to such effect, the expenses carry interest at such reasonable rate as the Council may determine from the date of service of that notice until the whole amount is paid and, subject to the following, the expenses and accrued interest are a charge on the premises (section 81A(1)). The notice must include details of the amount claimed and rate of interest charged by the Council. Reference must also be made to the person served with the notice having a right of appeal to the County Court within 21 days of the date of service. Copies of the notice must be served upon every other person who, to the knowledge of the Authority, has an interest in the premises.

For the purposes of section 81A the term "owner" in relation to any premises is defined as meaning:

> "a person (other than a mortgagee not in possession) who whether in his own right or as a trustee for any other person, is entitled to receive the rack rent of the premises or, where the premises are not let at a rack rent would be so entitled if they were so let,. . ."

A Local Authority shall for the purpose of enforcing a charge under this section have the same powers and remedies under the Law of Property Act 1925 as if it were a mortgagee by deed having powers of sale and lease, of accepting surrenders of leases and of appointing a receiver (section 81A(8)). Specific powers also granted to Authorities to take injunctive proceedings in the High Court notwithstanding the fact they have suffered no damage from the nuisance.

Appeals

A person served with an Abatement Notice may appeal against the notice to a Magistrates' Court within 21 days beginning with the date of service (section 80(3)). The 21 day time limit is strict and there is no provision for any extension of this time limit. Appeals are by way of complaint for an order and any appeal against a decision of the Magistrates lies to the Crown Court (Schedule 3 para 1). More detailed provisions relating to appeals are set out in the Statutory Nuisance (Appeals) Regulations 1990. In particular, the following grounds of appeal are prescribed:

(a) that the notice is not justified by section 80 of the Act;

(b) there has been some informality, defect or error in or in connection with the notice;

(c) that the authority have refused unreasonably to accept compliance with alternative requirements or that the requirements of the notice are otherwise unreasonable in character or extent or are unnecessary;

(d) that the period or periods for compliance with the notice are unreasonable;

(e) that the "best practicable means" provisions apply and such means have been used to prevent or counteract nuisance;

(f) in the case of a noise nuisance notice, the requirements exceed any pre-existing requirements of the Control of Pollution Act 1974;

(g) that the notice should have been served on some person instead of the appellant;

(h) where the Act gives the Authority a discretion upon whom to serve the notice that it would have been more equitable for it to have been served upon another party (e.g. an owner instead of an occupier or the person responsible for the nuisance instead of the owner, or vice versa).

Where an appeal is brought upon this last ground, the appellant must serve a copy of the notice of appeal on any other person referred to and may also serve a copy of the notice of appeal on any other person having an estate or interest in the premises.

If the appeal is based upon the ground of informality, defect or error in or in connection with the notice the court must dismiss the appeal if it is satisfied that the informality etc was not material.

Upon hearing an appeal, the court has a discretion to quash or vary the notice or dismiss the appeal.

Suspension of Notices Pending Determination of Appeals

An appeal to the Magistrates' Court will not operate to suspend the effect of the notice where:

- the nuisance in question is injurious to health or likely to be of such limited duration that suspension would render the notice ineffective; or
- any expenditure to be incurred in compliance with the notice prior to determination of the appeal would not be disproportionate to the public benefit to be expected in that period from such compliance; and
- the notice includes a statement to the effect that the above requirements have been met and the notice will remain in effect notwithstanding any appeal and confirming which of the above grounds apply.

Where the above requirements have not been met and compliance would involve expenditure prior to the hearing of the appeal (or in the case of a noise nuisance notice the noise is caused in the performance of a legal duty imposed on the appellant) the Abatement Notice is suspended until the appeal is abandoned or determined by the court (Regulation 3 of the 1990 Regulations).

Contaminated Land – the New Proposals

Key Points

- Duty on Councils to indentify contaminated land and prepare "remediation statements"
- Power to impose clean-up requirements
- Primarily aimed at polluters but possibility of non-polluting landowners being held responsible
- Exemption for insolvency practitioners

The Environment Bill published on 1 December 1994, in addition to proposing the establishment of the Environment Agency to take over the functions of the NRA, HMIP and Waste Regulation Authorities, proposes the introduction of a new regime, analogous to the statutory nuisance regime in certain respects, for the identification and remediation of closed landfill sites and other contaminated land. The Bill, as and when enacted, will amend the 1990 Act by adding a new Part IIA with sections numbered 78A to 78P.

"Contaminated land" is defined as any land which appears to the relevant Local Authority to be in such a condition by reason of substances in, on or under the land that harm or pollution of controlled waters is being or is likely to be caused. The term "controlled waters" is given the same extensive definition as in the Water Resources Act 1991, i.e. it includes ground waters (see Chapter 3). The term "closed landfill site" is defined as any contaminated land which appears to the Local Authority to be land which does not benefit from a waste disposal or waste management licence but upon which:

(a) controlled waste has been deposited in the past under the provisions of such a licence; or

(b) controlled waste has been deposited without the benefit of a licence or in contravention of such a licence (but disregarding household waste deposited within the curtilage of dwelling and deposits which would be exempted from control by virtue of regulations to be made by the Secretary of State) (section 78A).

The new provisions will place a duty upon Local Authorities (District Councils, London Boroughs and new Unitary Authorities) to inspect their areas to for the purpose of identifying contaminated land, closed landfill sites and sites suitable for designation as "special sites" (i.e. closed landfill sites designated by the Secretary of State as presenting risks of serious harm or serious pollution of controlled waters).

Local Authorities are to be given a further duty to prepare "remediation statements" in respect of closed landfill sites, other than special sites which will be the responsibility of the new Environment Agency (section 78C). The remediation statement must specify:

(a) what is required to assess the condition of:
  – the contaminated land in question
  – any controlled waters affected by that land; or
  – any adjacent land;
(b) works, operations and steps required in relation to such land or waters for the purpose of:
  – preventing, minimising, remedying or mitigating the effects of any harm or pollution; or
  – restoring the land or waters to their former state; or
(c) future monitoring of the land or waters.

The proposals then go on to make provision for the Agency or Local Authority concerned to serve remediation notices upon the appropriate person in respect of contaminated land specifying what they are required to do by way of remediation within a specified timescale (s 78D).

The new regime also contains specific provisions dealing with migrating contamination. A person who has caused or knowingly permitted contamination of land shall also be taken to have caused or knowingly permitted that contamination to be in, on or under any other land to which they appear to have escaped. However, no remediation notice can require remedial work where the owner or occupier appears not to have caused the substance in question to be present upon their land, e.g. where they have migrated from elsewhere and migrated onto another innocent third party's land (section 78F). At the time of going to press these provisions are in a state of flux.

Who is Served
The proposed legislation is aimed at making the person who caused the contamination primarily responsible for remediation (section 78E(2)). Where no such person can be found, the appropriate person will be the owner or occupier for the time being of the contaminated land in question

(section 78E(3)). Similarly, where liability is transferred from the polluter to the owner or occupier for the time being, the remediation notice should be served upon that owner or occupier (section 78E(3)(b)). However, the concept of transferral of liability is not elaborated upon in the Bill.

Where the person responsible for the contamination is not in occupation of the contaminated land he may not be served with a remediation notice unless the occupier gives his written consent to the polluter to carry out required works (sections 78D(4) and 78(E)(3(c)). This presupposes the existence of a notice laying down requirements albeit that it has yet to be served upon the person responsible. The Bill makes reference to procedures yet to be prescribed.

Additionally, where a notice may be served on more than one person or may be served upon an owner or occupier, authorities are instructed to act in accordance with guidance to be issued by the Secretary of State in determining who is to be served with the remediation notice.

Contents of Remediation Notice

In specifying its requirements relating to remediation, restoration and monitoring, the authority must only specify things it considers reasonable having regard to cost and the seriousness of harm or pollution. In determining the requirements specified in a remediation notice and the standard to which any land or waters are to be remediated the authority must have regard to guidance issued by the new Agency or the Secretary of State (section 78D(2) and (5)). Early indications from the Department of the Environment point to the guidance adopting a "fitness for purpose" approach, i.e. the land should be remediated so that it is fit for its likely future use, as opposed to the approach adopted in the US of attempting to remove all contamination from affected sites.

A remediation notice cannot be served if it appears to the authority that it is appropriate for the Chief Inspector of HMIP to exercise his clean-up powers pursuant to the IPC regime (see Chapter 2 below).

Appeals against Remediation Notices

A person upon whom a remediation notice is served has a period of 21 days beginning with the date of service in which to appeal. In the case of notices served by the Local Authority appeal lies to the Magistrates' Court. In the case of notices served by the Environment Agency appeal lies to the Secretary of State (section 78G(1)). The Magistrates and the Secretary of State have power to quash notices or to confirm with or without modification. Regulations are to be made with respect to grounds of appeal and procedure.

Enforcement and Clean-Up Powers

If a person upon whom a notice has been served fails to comply with its requirements he shall be guilty of a summary offence. Where the offence takes place on industrial, trade or business premises the maximum fine is £20,000 or such greater sum as the Secretary of State may substitute by order. In other cases the maximum fine is level 5 on the standard scale. If the notice is not complied with after first conviction, further fines may be imposed of up to one-tenth of the maximum fine for each day the offence continues. This "continuing offence" fine cannot be imposed in respect of a period following an authority's exercise of its clean-up powers (see below) (section 78H).

Where a notice is not complied with the enforcing authority may carry out remedial works itself and recover its reasonable costs from the person served with the notice. In determining whether or not to recover its costs and, if so, how much to recover the authority must have regard to any hardship which may be caused (section 78J(1) and (2)).

If costs are recoverable from an owner who caused or knowingly permitted the contamination to take place the authority can serve a further notice (a charging notice) which will result in the authority's costs and interest thereon being a charge on the premises. There are provisions enabling appeal against such charging notices (section 78J(3) to (13)).

Unlike some other parts of the EPA, the term "owner" is given a definition:

"a person (other than a mortgagee not in possession) who whether in his own right or as trustee for any other person is entitled to receive the rack rent of the land, or, where the land is not let at a rack rent would be so entitled if it were so let".

As mentioned in other chapters, where other statutory regimes adopt just such a definition, the definition is wide enough to include mortgagees in possession and receivers. However, the new proposals contain an important exemption for insolvency practitioners. They shall only be personally liable under the contaminated land regime to the extent that harm or pollution of controlled waters or the condition of land is attributable to their negligence (section 78P(3)). It appears that the Bill intends that lay Magistrates be given the function of considering civil law concepts such as negligence and the transfer of civil liabilities.

There is a question mark over whether or not an LPA receiver will benefit from the exemption granted to "insolvency practitioners". Unfortunately, the term is hitherto undefined in the Bill.

CHAPTER 2

Air Pollution and Integrated Pollution Control

Key Points

- A rolling programme of pollution control being introduced for the most problematic industries
- An ever stricter regime dealing with management methods as well as hardware provision
- Regularly updated guidance as to best practice
- Public access to information held by regulators
- Greater likelihood of enforcement action than under previous systems

The industrial processes most likely to give rise to serious pollution problems are governed by Her Majesty's Inspectorate of Pollution through the Integrated Pollution Control regime introduced by Part I of the Environmental Protection Act 1990. This regime also gives HMIP power to deal with emissions to water and to land as well as air emissions. Air pollution from a second tier of less polluting processes is policed by Local Authorities (see Appendices 1 and 2).

Section 6 of the EPA prohibits the carrying on of a prescribed process except in accordance with an authorisation granted by the relevant enforcing authority. Applications must be either granted subject to conditions pursuant to section 7 (see below), or refused. An application must be refused unless the authority considers that the applicant will be able to carry on the process in compliance with the conditions imposed (section 6(4)). The Secretary of State may give directions as to how particular applications should be dealt with (section 6(5)). Conditions imposed in authorisations must be reviewed at least every four years or such other period of time as specified by the Secretary of State (section 6(6) and (7)).

Authorisations must contain such conditions as are prescribed by the Secretary of State and such other conditions as appear appropriate to the enforcing authority. Additionally, and most importantly, conditions must be imposed to ensure that in carrying on a prescribed process the best available techniques not entailing excessive cost ("BATNEEC") will be used to prevent the release of prescribed substances or, where that is not practicable, for reducing such releases to a minimum and rendering them harmless (section 7).

Best Available Techniques

The first point to note is that, unlike comparable European legislation, the BATNEEC requirement relates to "techniques" and not just technology or equipment. The term is wide enough to include the manner in which activities are carried out, i.e. managerial techniques as well as matters of hardware provision and design. Guidance issued by the Department of the Environment states that it also includes matters such as numbers and qualifications of staff, working methods, training and supervision, as well as the design construction, layout and maintenance of buildings (*Integrated Pollution Control – A Practical Guide* – DoE).

A degree of judgement is required with regard to whether or not any particular technique is "available". Availability is not limited to the UK and includes, for example, hardware which can only be obtained from monopoly suppliers. The question appears to be – is a technique generally accessible to the operator?

If one set of techniques is more effective than others in preventing, minimising or rendering harmless polluting emissions then it will be the "best" for the purposes of the Act. However, if a number of techniques achieve comparable effectiveness, then there may be more than one set of techniques which are "best".

Not Entailing Excessive Cost

With new processes, there will be a presumption that best available techniques will be employed. However, that presumption is rebuttable if the costs would be excessive in relating to the nature of the industry and the degree of environmental protection which will be achieved.

With regard to existing processes, it is quite conceivable that certain facilities will be incapable of being upgraded and may have to be decommissioned. The EC Air Framework Directive requires the imposition of appropriate conditions in authorisations not only on the basis of developments with regard to BAT but also on the basis of the desirability of avoiding excessive costs for the operators in question having regard to the economic circumstances of the industrial sector concerned. The Directive goes on to require Member States to implement the policies and strategies for the gradual adaptation of existing plant to the best available technology taking into account the plant's technical characteristics, its remaining life, the nature and volume of emissions and the desirability of not entailing excessive costs for the plant concerned having particular regard to the economic situation of the type of undertaking. Guidance notes are issued by HMIP before any particular process is brought within IPC giving detailed advice on BATNEEC in specific instances.

The enforcing authority may at any time vary the conditions attached to an authorisation. A "Variation Notice" must be served upon the holder of the authorisation specifying the variations and the date or dates upon which they are to take effect. The notice must also require the holder to notify the authority of what action (if any) he proposes to take to ensure that the process is carried on in accordance with the variation. The notice may also require payment of a fee. The Secretary of State has powers to direct enforcing authorities to vary authorisations.

Additionally, the holder of an authorisation wishing to change the manner in which he carries out a process in a manner capable of altering the substance's release or the amount or any other characteristic of a released substance may request the enforcing authority to vary the conditions of the authorisation (section11).

Enforcing authorities are given a very general power to revoke authorisations. The power to revoke is expressed without limitation or reservation although section 12(2) makes reference to circumstances where an authority believes that a process for which an authorisation is in force has not been carried out for a period of 12 months. The Secretary of State can direct authorities to revoke authorisations.

If the enforcing authority believes that the holder of an authorisation is contravening or likely to contravene a condition, the authority may serve an Enforcement Notice. The power to issue such a notice is discretionary. The notice must specify the contravention or anticipated contravention, the steps necessary to remedy the situation and a period within which those steps must be taken (section 13).

If the authority believes that the continued operation of a process pursuant to an authorisation involves an imminent risk of serious pollution of the environment, it *must* serve (i.e. it is under a statutory duty to serve) a "Prohibition Notice" on the person carrying on the process. The notice must specify the risk involved, the steps that must be taken to remove it, the period within which they must be taken and direct that the authorisation shall cease to have effect until such time as the notice is withdrawn. The notice can also impose conditions upon the carrying on of parts of a process (section 14). The Secretary of State has powers to direct authorities to issue enforcement and prohibition notices.

Appeals may be made to the Secretary of State against:

- refusals of applications for authorisation;
- conditions attached to authorisations;
- refusals of variations applied for;
- Enforcement and Prohibition Notices;
- revocations of authorisations.

The Secretary of State may affirm the decision of the enforcing authority or in appropriate cases direct the authority to grant or vary authorisations. Alternatively, the Secretary of State may quash authorities' decisions and may direct that conditions be attached to authorisations.

Where an appeal is brought against a revocation of an authorisation, that revocation does not take effect until final determination or withdrawal of the appeal. Where an appeal is made against a Variation Notice, Enforcement Notice or Prohibition Notice, the operation of the Notice is not suspended by the appeal. Detailed procedure is contained in the Environmental Protection (Applications, Appeals and Registers) Regulations 1991.

Authorisations may be transferred by the holder to the person who proposes to carry on the process in the holder's place. The transferee must notify the enforcing authority in writing of the transfer within 21 days of the date of transfer (section 9).

Public Registers

Enforcing authorities are under a duty to maintain a register containing particulars of the following matters:

- applications for authorisations;
- authorisations granted;
- Variation Notices, Enforcement Notices and Prohibition Notices;
- Revocations, Appeals;
- convictions;
- information obtained or furnished pursuant to conditions imposed and authorisations or pursuant to the authorities' statutory powers;
- directions issued by the Secretary of State.

The Secretary of State has the power to exclude information from a register on the grounds of national security. Additionally, persons furnishing information to an authority for the purposes of applying for an authorisation or complying with the condition or notice may apply to the authority to have information excluded on the grounds of commercial confidentiality (see sections 20-22).

Criminal Liability

It is a criminal offence to:

(a) operate a prescribed process without an authorisation or in contravention of conditions (section 6(1));

(b) to fail to give notice of a transfer of an authorisation (section 9(2));

(c) to fail to comply with an Enforcement Notice or Prohibition Notice;

(d) to fail to co-operate with Inspectors in the execution of their function (section 17);

(e) to prevent any other person from appearing before or answering questions to which an Inspector may require an answer (section 17(3));

(f) intentionally to obstruct an Inspector in the performance of his functions;

(g) to fail, without reasonable excuse, to comply with the requirements of notices requiring information (section 19(2));

(h) to knowingly make false or misleading statements or to recklessly make such statements or where the statement is made in purported compliance with a requirement to furnish information or for the purpose of obtaining authorisation or variation of an authorisation;

(i) intentionally to make false entries in statutory records;
(j) to forge or use statutory documents with intent to deceive or to have in one's possession a document so closely resembling such a document as to be likely to deceive;
(k) to impersonate an Inspector; and
(l) to fail to comply with a Court Order requiring remedial works (section 26).

Offences are triable either way. An offence under paragraphs (a), (c) and (l) above are punishable on summary conviction by a fine not exceeding £20,000 and on conviction on indictment to an unlimited fine and/or a term of imprisonment of up to two years. Offences under (b), (g), (h), (i) and (j) above are punishable on summary conviction by a fine not exceeding a statutory maximum and on conviction upon indictment to an unlimited fine and/or a term of imprisonment of up to two years. The remaining offences (largely administrative matters) are only triable summarily and punishable by a fine not exceeding the statutory maximum.

If the enforcing authority is of the opinion that prosecution through the Magistrates' Court or the Crown Court for failure to comply with an Enforcement Notice or a Prohibition Notice would afford an ineffectual remedy, it may take proceedings in the High Court for an injunction. As well as providing a more expeditious remedy non-compliance with an injunction may also lead to contempt proceedings (section 24). In proceedings relating to paragraph (a) above consisting in the failure to comply with BATNEEC the onus of proof is on the defendant to demonstrate that there was no better technique available not entailing excessive costs than was in fact used (section 25).

Clean-Up Powers

Where a person is convicted of an offence under (a) or (c) above, ie operating without an authorisation or contravening an Enforcement Notice or a Prohibition Notice or conditions the court can in addition to or instead of imposing a punishment order the defendant to take remedial measures within a specified time limit (section 26). Additionally, the Chief Inspector of HMIP can, with the approval of the Secretary of State and with the permission of the occupier of any land affected, (other than the land upon which the prescribed process is being carried on) carry out remedial works and recover the costs from any convicted defendant (section 27).

Where an offence is committed by a body corporate and is proved to have been committed with the consent or connivance of, or to have been attributable to, any neglect on the part of any director, manager, secretary or other similar officer of the body corporate (or a person purporting to act in such capacity) he, as well as the body corporate, shall be guilty of that offence. If the affairs of the body corporate are managed by its members these provisions apply to individual members as if they were directors of the body corporate (section 157).

Where the commission of an offence is due to the act or default of some other person that other person may be charged with and convicted of the offence whether or not proceedings are taken against the first mentioned person (section 158).

Clean Air Act 1993

Parts I and II lay down criminal sanctions for the emission of "dark smoke from premises" and the emission of smoke, grit, dust and fumes from furnaces. These criminal sanctions are directed towards the occupiers of premises and persons who install furnaces in contravention of the Act's requirements. Exemptions are set out for processes which are subject to IPC control, mines and quarries, railway engines, vessels and processes governed by the Alkali and Works Act 1906.

Part III of the Act contains the provisions for designation of smoke control areas by local authorities and the powers of the Secretary of State to direct the designation of such areas. Once again criminal sanctions are directed towards the occupiers of premises which emit smoke in contravention of such orders. Additional sanctions are directed towards persons who acquire or supply solid fuel for use in premises in contravention of a smoke control order.

Part IV of the Act gives the Secretary of State the power to make regulations governing the composition of fuel to be used in motor vehicles and to impose limits on the sulphur content of oil fuel used in furnaces or engines (sections 30 and 31). No regulations have been made under this section but regulations made under earlier legislation (the Motor Fuel (Sulphur Content of Gas Oil) Regulations 1976 and the Motor Fuel (Lead Content of Petrol) Regulations 1981 and the Oil Fuel (Sulphur Content of Gas Oil) Regulations 1990) remain in force by virtue of the Interpretation Act 1978. Part IV of the Act also prohibits the practice of cable burning.

CHAPTER 3

Water Pollution

Key Points

- Comprehensive range of criminal penalties
- Clean-up powers issued at polluters as opposed to landowners or occupiers
- Rigorous and vigorous enforcement

Criminal Liability

Section 85 of the Water Resources Act 1991 creates a wide range of offences relating to the pollution of controlled waters. The term "controlled waters" is given a very wide definition and includes inland fresh waters, groundwaters, coastal waters and relevant territorial waters (all of which terms are further defined in section 104). By virtue of section 85(1), a person commits an offence if he causes or knowingly permits any poisonous, noxious or polluting matter or any solid waste matter to enter any controlled waters.

The question of causation was considered by a strong Queen's Bench Division in *Wychavon District Council* v *NRA* (1992). In that case it was held that in order to prove a charge of causing pollution the NRA would have to demonstrate either a positive or deliberate act on the defendant's part. Mere negligence would be insufficient. The court in *Wychavon* were to a large extent guided by the House of Lords decision in *Alphacell Limited* v *Woodward* (1972). In that case, Lord Wilberforce stated:

"...causing...must involve some active operation or chain of operations involving as a result the pollution of the stream; knowingly permitting...involves a failure to prevent the pollution which failure, however, must be accompanied by knowledge."

Section 85(1) refers to "poisonous, noxious or polluting matter" and it is clear that these three alternative are not synonymous. In *NRA* v *Egger (UK) Limited* (1992) a Crown Court was of the opinion that polluting matter was such as to be "capable of causing harm in that it may damage a river's potential usefulness" and covered "harm to animal, vegetable or other life in a river and/or aesthetic damage". It is clear that something further is required with regard to poisonous or noxious discharges (see *Schulmans Inc* v *NRA* (1992)).

Sub-sections (2) to (4) create similar offences relating to drains and sewers and trade effluent. Sub-section (5) deals with matters entering inland fresh waters which impede proper flow or causing substantial aggravation. All offences under section 85 are triable either way. On summary conviction defendants are liable to a term of imprisonment not exceeding three months and/or a fine of up to £20,000. On conviction on indictment, defendants are liable to up to two years' imprisonment and/or an unlimited fine.

The Act provides specific defences to charges under section 85 (see sections 88 and 89). These include acts or omissions in accordance with specific statutory consents. Furthermore, a person shall not be guilty if the discharge was made:

- in an emergency to avoid danger to life or health;
- by someone taking all steps as are reasonably practicable for minimising the discharge and its effect; and
- particulars are furnished to the NRA as soon as reasonably practicable.

Clean-Up Powers

Section 161 of the WRA provides that if any poisonous, noxious or polluting matter or solid waste has entered or is likely to enter controlled waters the NRA can carry out certain specified anti-pollution works and recover their expenses from the person who caused or knowingly permitted the pollutant to be present in the controlled waters or to be at a place where it was likely to enter them.

Where the pollutant appears likely to enter controlled waters, the NRA can reclaim its expenses for preventative works and operations. Where the pollutant already appears to be in the controlled waters, they may claim their expenses in respect of works and operations for:

- removing or disposing of the matter;
- remedying or mitigating any pollution caused; or
- restoring the waters, including flora and fauna dependant on the aquatic environment to the state immediately before the pollution incident so far as reasonably practicable.

On a strict interpretation of the above, it would appear that the NRA has no power to reclaim under this provision in respect of works which are purely investigative.

Expenses which fall within the limitations of section 161 and which are reasonably incurred may be recovered from any person who either caused or knowingly permitted the pollutant to be present at a place from which it was likely in the opinion of the Authority to enter the controlled waters or who caused or knowingly permitted the pollutant to be so present. The powers granted by section 161 are additional to the usual civil rights of action and criminal penalties.

Expenses arising in connection with pollution or potential pollution from abandoned mines is irrecoverable under section 161.

Trade Effluent

Discharges of trade effluent into public sewers are governed by Chapter III of Part IV of the Water Industry Act 1991. The consent of the relevant sewerage undertaker is required for such discharges. The occupier of any trade premises who discharges to a public sewer without consent is guilty of an offence. Such offences committed by the occupier, are triable either way and punishable on summary conviction by a fine not exceeding the statutory maximum and conviction on indictment to a fine (section 118). In granting a consent a sewage undertaker may impose conditions relating to the nature, composition, quantity and rate of discharges (section 121). Any person aggrieved by a refusal or non-determination of an application or by any condition imposed by any consent may appeal to the Director General of Water Services (section 122). Sewage undertakers may from time to time vary the conditions attached to a consent (section 124). Slightly different procedures exist with regard to "special category" effluent (i.e. effluent comprising particularly dangerous substances). Lists of such effluent are prescribed by the Trade Effluent (Prescribed Processes and Substances) Regulations 1989 and the Trade Effluent (Prescribed Processes and Substances) (Amendment) Regulations 1990.

CHAPTER 4

Waste on Land

Key Points

- New statutory duty of care for all waste producers
- Tighter licencing regime to encourage better operational practice and prevent abandonement of sites
- Operation to be "fit and proper" and financially capable of remedying likely problems

Criminal Liabilities

Section 33 of the Environmental Protection Act 1990 makes it an offence to deposit or knowingly cause or knowingly permit controlled waste to be deposited on land unless it is done in accordance with the provisions of waste management licence. It is also an offence to treat, keep or dispose of controlled waste in a manner likely to cause pollution to the environment or harm to human health. The term "controlled waste" is defined as meaning household, industrial or commercial waste (section 75 (4)). The terms "household waste", "industrial waste" and "commercial waste" are further defined by section 75 (5) to (7).

The term "pollution to the environment" is defined by section 29 to mean pollution of the environment (i.e. land, water and the air) due to the release or escape from land or plant or on by means of which controlled waste is treated, kept or deposited, of substances or articles constituting or resulting from the waste and capable of causing harm to man or other living organisms.

The above general criminal provisions do not apply to household waste from a domestic property which is treated, kept or disposed of within the curtilage of the dwelling by or with the permission of its occupier (section 33 (2)). The Secretary of State for the Environment has the power to exclude other activities from the general criminal provisions.

Offences are triable either way and are punishable on summary conviction to a term of imprisonment of up to six months and/or a fine of up to £20,000. On indictment offences are punishable by a term not exceeding two years and/or an unlimited fine. Where an offence relates to waste which is designated by regulations made by the Secretary of State as "special waste" (i.e. particularly dangerous waste) the maximum term of imprisonment is five years.

Section 33 (7) provides a specific statutory defence if the person charged can prove:

- that he took all reasonable precautions and exercised all due diligence to avoid commission of the offence; or
- that he acted under instructions from his employer and neither knew nor had reason to suppose that his acts constituted an offence; or
- that the acts in question were done in an emergency to avoid danger to the public and particulars were furnished to the Waste Regulation Authority as soon as reasonably practicable.

Duty of Care

Section 34 (1) of the EPA imposes a new duty upon all persons importing, producing, carrying, keeping, treating or disposing of controlled waste or who as broker control such waste to take all measures applicable to him as are reasonable:

- to prevent contravention by any other person of the general criminal provisions contained in section 33 (above);
- to prevent escape of waste from his or anybody else's control; and
- on the transfer of waste to secure:
  (i) that the transfer is to an authorised person or a person authorised for transport purposes; and
  (ii) that a written description of the waste is also transferred to enable other persons to avoid contravention of section 33 and also to enable them to comply with the duty relating to escape of waste above.

These duties do not apply to domestic occupiers as respects household waste produced on their property.

The term "authorised person" includes the holders of waste management licences (see below), registered carriers under the Control of Pollution (Amendment) Act 1989 and waste collection authorities (i.e. usually the District Council) as well as persons exempted by regulations to be made by the Secretary of State (section 34 (3)).

Failure to comply with the duty of care is an either way offence punishable on summary conviction by a fine not exceeding the statutory maximum or on indictment to an unlimited fine. The Secretary of State for the Environment is under an obligation to produce a code of practice to provide practical guidance on how the duty should be discharged (section 34 (7)). The code of practice is admissible in evidence and if any provision appears relevant to the court it must be taken into account in determining any questions arising in the proceedings (section 34 10)).

Waste Licensing

This work is primarily concerned with questions of liability and not matters of licensing procedure. However, given the importance of the presence or absence of a licence with regard to many questions of criminal liability arising under sections 33 and 34 practitioners may wish to peruse sections 35 to 44 of the EPA which deal with applications for licences and the functions of waste regulation authorities in this respect. Additionally section 74 deals with the important question of who is or is not a "fit and proper person" for the purposes of these licensing provisions.

The following features of the licensing regime should be noted:

- a licence will not be issued unless a planning permission, established use certificate or certificate of lawful use has been issued under the Planning Acts (section 36 (2));
- licences may only be surrendered to the authority in limited circumstances. In summary, the authority must be satisfied that the condition of the land is unlikely to cause pollution of the environment or harm to human health. Unless the authority is so satisfied, it must refuse the surrender. If an authority is minded to accept a surrender, it must first refer the matter to the NRA. If the NRA requests that the surrender be refused, either body may refer

the matter to the Secretary of State and the question of surrender may only be determined in accordance with his decision (section 39);

- prima facie, licences are not transferable by the holder. However, licensees and proposed transferees may make joint application to the waste regulation authority for transfer. If the authority is satisfied that the proposed transferee is a fit and proper person, it must effect the transfer (section 40);
- licence applications must be referred to both the NRA and the HSE. Any disagreement upon the application or proposed conditions may be referred to any of the authorities by the Secretary of State. In such circumstances the licence can only be issued in accordance with his decision.

If applications remain undetermined for a period of four months (or such longer period as is agreed between the parties) the authority is deemed to have rejected the application. Appeals lie to the Secretary of State for the Environment.

- licences may be varied either on an authority's own initiative (if, in the opinion of the authority the variation is desirable and unlikely to require unreasonable expense on the holder's part) and on the application of the licence holder;
- licences may be revoked or suspended if:
  (i) the licence holder has ceased to be a fit and proper person by reason of committing specified offences;
  (ii) the continuation of the authorised activities would cause pollution of the environment or harm to human health or would be seriously detrimental to local amenities and such pollution, harm or detriment cannot be avoided by modifying the licence conditions;
  (iii) the licence holder has ceased to be a fit and proper person by reason of the management of the authorised activities ceasing to be in the hands of a technically competent person (see section 38).

The concept of "fit and proper person" is a new one and the provisions of section 74 remain, at present, largely untested. A person shall be treated as being not fit and proper if it appears to the authority that he or certain associates of the applicant or licensee have been convicted of a relevant offence (see section 74(3)(a) and (7)).

- that the management of the proposed activities will not be in the hands of a technically competent person; or
- that the person who holds or is to hold the licence has not made and either has no intention of making or is not in a position to make adequate financial provision to discharge the obligations arising from the licence.

It is open to an authority to waive a conviction in determining whether or not the person is fit and proper. Regulations are to be made setting out the qualifications and experience required in determining whether or not a person is technically competent. The question of financial provision is essentially more problematic. The potential criminal, civil and clean-up costs which may arise from, say, the migration of gases or leaching of liquids from landfill sites can be extremely expensive. At present the insurance industry appears to be concentrating its efforts upon limiting the quantum and period of cover available for such incidents. The number of operators able to make the necessary financial provision without the benefit of insurance is extremely limited.

Schedule 3 to the Waste Management Licensing Regulations 1994 contains a lengthy list of activities which are exempt from these licensing provisions.

Clean-Up Powers

Section 61 of the EPA grants waste regulation authorities extensive clean up functions. [At the time of going to press this section has not been brought into force and if the current Environment Bill is passed the section will be repeated – see contaminated land provisions in Chapter 1.]

At first glance it appears that section 61 is intended to deal with closed landfill sites. The sub- heading in the Act reads "duty of waste regulation authorities as respects closed landfills". However, the wording of the section goes far further. First of all it imposes a general duty of inspection upon the authority: "a duty to cause their areas to be inspected to detect whether *any land* is in such a condition by reason of relevant matters that it may cause pollution of the environment or harm to human health". The term "relevant matters" is defined to include such things as concentrations, accumulations, emissions or discharges of noxious gases or liquids caused by deposits of controlled waste.

The section then goes on to provide that where it appears that the condition of *any land* is such that pollution or harm is likely to arise, it is the *duty* of the authority to do such works and to take such other steps (whether on the land affected or on adjacent land) as appear to be reasonable to avoid such pollution or harm. It will be noted that there is no requirement that the harm either arises upon or is caused by or to a landfill site closed or otherwise. Deposits of controlled waste giving rise to "relevant matters" can occur not only within landfill sites (open or closed) but within the boundary of most industrial undertakings and may even be caused by trespassers or arise from uses long since ceased.

Where an authority exercises its duty under section 61 the authority is entitled (except in limited circumstances) to recover its costs from the owner of the land for the time being. Unfortunately, the term "owner" remains undefined in the EPA. This point is debated in Chapter 1 above.

Statutory Civil Liability

By virtue of section 73 (6) where any damage is caused by waste which has been deposited in or on land anybody who deposited it or knowingly caused or permitted its deposit thereby committing an offence under section 33 (unauthorised deposit of controlled waste) or section 63 (2) (unauthorised deposit of special waste) is strictly liable for that damage unless it was due wholly to the fault of the person who suffered it or was suffered by someone who voluntarily accepted the risk of the damage being caused. This provision is stated to be without prejudice to any other liability arising. A defence may also be claimed if the matters referred to in section 33 (7) can be demonstrated (see above).

Litter

Part IV of the EPA contains a combination of criminal penalties and administrative provisions for dealing with litter and abandoned shopping and luggage trolleys. section 87 contains the basic prohibition against the dropping of litter in, into or from:

- Public open spaces
- Highways
- Council-owned land
- Relevant Crown lands
- Relevant land of statutory undertakers
- Relevant land of educational institutions
- Relevant land within a "litter controlled area" (section 87(1) to (3)).

Contravention is a summary offence punishable by a fine not exceeding level 4 on the standard scale.

Authorised Officers of Councils (and National Park Officers) have the power to issue fixed penalty notices to persons they have reason to believe have committed a littering offence. The person served may pay a fixed penalty of £10 (subject to review by the Secretary of State) as an alternative to being prosecuted (section 88). The Act imposes a duty upon Local Authorities to keep relevant roads and other open land which they control free from litter. This duty is extended to the Secretary of State for Transport as regards trunk roads, Crown Authorities as regards Crown land and statutory undertakers as regards open land controlled by them. Additionally, the duty applies to occupiers of open land within a litter control area, i.e. land so designated by a District Council or London Borough in accordance with the statutory procedure laid down in section 90 (see also section 89).

Private individuals aggrieved by the littering of highways, trunk roads, Council land etc, may apply by complaint to the Magistrates for an Order (a "Litter Abatement Order") requiring the Authority in question or the occupier of the land to clear the litter or refuse in question. Non-compliance with a Litter Abatement Order is a summary offence punishable by a fine not exceeding level 4 on the standard scale (section 91). In determining the standard of cleanliness required regard is to be had to codes of practice issued by the Department of the Environment.

District Councils and London Boroughs are given powers to serve "Litter Abatement Notices" upon the occupiers of open land within litter controlled areas, Crown land, statutory undertakers' land and the land of designated educational institutions requiring clearance of litter and refuse within specified time limits. The person served may appeal to the Magistrates' Court within 21 days of service. Non-compliance with notices is a summary offence punishable by a fine not exceeding level 4 on the standard scale.

CHAPTER 5

Common Law Civil Liability

Spillages, migrations and other incidents of pollution have always given rise to private actions by aggrieved parties pursuant to the common law rules relating to nuisance, negligence, *Rylands* v *Fletcher* and trespass. This is not the place to examine, let alone go into the details of, the fundamental nature of those common law torts. The published works dealing with common law actions are well known. The following parts of this chapter deal with how the courts have dealt with tortious actions arising from environmental incidents in recent years. Given the topicality environmental issues within the legal profession, pressure groups and, perhaps to a lesser extent, industrial operators it might be regarded as surprising that more actions have not been pursued through the civil courts. This could be a reflection of the degree of uncertainty which has existed with regard to the law in this area. That uncertainty has now been substantially remedied by the House of Lords decision in *Cambridge Water Company Limited* v *Eastern Counties Leather Plc*.

The Cambridge Water Case

Key Points

- No liability in nuisance or *Rylands* v *Fletcher* where damage cannot be foreseen
- Where damage is reasonably forseeable liability will be strict
- Courts reluctant to impose retrospective liability

The *Cambridge Water* case has attracted substantial attention in the mainstream business press as well as the usual legal journals. The case concerned chemical pollution to ground water supplies caused by a tannery. Tannery processes had been carried on in the village in question for over 350 years. Spillages of chemicals had occurred as an almost inevitable result of the tannery processes. These spillages then percolated down into the ground waters from which the water company drew its supplies. All concerned had been aware of the pollution for very many years but no action was taken due to the level of pollutants within the ground waters falling within EC limits. The EC then tightened its limits to the extent that they were acceded by the level of pollutants then present, although the offending spillages had ceased some years previously. The Water Company then commenced action (pursuant to nuisance, negligence and *Rylands* v *Fletcher*).

At first instance, Ian Kennedy J, in a very detailed and thorough judgment, held that the use of organocholorines in a useful and 350 year old trade within an industrial village did not attract the label "non-natural" and therefore the rule in *Rylands* v *Fletcher* was inapplicable.

As regards nuisance or negligence the first question to address was what consequences were reasonably foreseeable as a result of the spillages? There must be some relationship between the harm to be foreseen and the harm occurring. The correct test to apply was – what would the reasonable supervisor overseeing the operation of the plant have foreseen to be the possible consequence of repeated spillages over perhaps ten years? He may have foreseen harm from one large spillage but that was not the proper question. The reasonable supervisor alive to a pattern of lesser spillages, as occurred upon Eastern counties land, would not foresee any environmental hazard.

As regards both the nuisance and the negligence claim, actual damage was necessary to sustain the cause of action. Here any proof of damage only arose upon the introduction of new EC regulations and postdated the spillages in question by many years. If there was evidence of continuing spillages an injunction would have been granted to restrain that continuance. However, there should be no award of damages in respect of the current impact of actions that were not actionable nuisances or negligence when committed 15 years previously. Any clean up liability or payment of damages must be a matter for Parliament and not the common law.

Not surprisingly the matter went to appeal. There was no appeal to the Court of Appeal on the judge's findings in nuisance and negligence but Cambridge Water appealed on his finding on *Rylands* v *Fletcher*. Like Kennedy before them the Court of Appeal was guided substantially by 19th century authorities. The Court classed the water company's right to draw water from the aquifer as a "natural" right and based their decision upon the case of *Ballard* v *Tomlinson* (1885).

In that case the Plaintiff and Defendant were adjacent land owners who each owned a well sunk into a chalk aquifer. The Plaintiff pumped water from his well for the purposes of his brewery. However the Defendant used his well as a receptacle for sewage and other effluent from his printing works. The Court of Appeal in Ballard found for the plaintiff and in the *Cambridge Water* case the Court found the facts to be "scarcely distinguishable" and Kennedy was wrong not to apply it. The fact that in *Cambridge Water* the Appellant and the Respondent were not adjacent land owners was immaterial as the same aquifer was beneath the surface of each ownership. It was also immaterial that Tomlinson's effluent was deliberately put into his well whilst Eastern Counties' contaminants were spilt by accident. It was sufficient that the Defendant's act caused the contamination. The Respondent's inability to foresee that the spillages would have the consequences they did was also irrelevant. The Court was not concerned with the Defendant's state of actual or imputed knowledge. The situation was one in which negligence played no part. The Court of Appeal allowed Cambridge Water's appeal finding that there was strict liability in damages for the contamination of the water.

Ballard v *Tomlinson* was good authority for the proposition that when a nuisance is an interference with a natural right incident to ownership then liability is strict. The actor acts at his peril in that if his actions result by the operation of ordinary natural processes in an interference with the right then he is liable to compensate for any damaged caused. No importance was attached to the fact that the water company suffered damage only when quality standards were raised and indeed some years after the spillage had ceased.

The Court went on to say that their conclusions on the point of nuisance made it unnecessary to consider questions relating to the rules in *Rylands* v *Fletcher* however they thought that the rule was inappropriate in the present case. *Rylands* v *Fletcher* makes a person liable for the event of an escape rather than his actions. The *Cambridge Water* case was one where liability arose by reason of the actions of the Respondent in spilling contaminants. Had the chemical escaped into the aquifer through cracks in a storage tank which had been negligently fabricated by an apparently competent contractor then the case would have required an examination of *Rylands* v *Fletcher*. The Court went on to say that they doubted whether the original *Rylands* v *Fletcher* decision required that the thing which escaped must have been brought onto the Defendant's land in the course of a "non-natural" use.

The case finally went to the House of Lords. Despite the fact that there was no appeal by the Water Company to the Court of Appeal against the judge's conclusion in nuisance, the House of Lords decided that since there was a close relationship between nuisance and the rule in *Rylands* v *Fletcher*, it was necessary to look at the nature of liability in relation to both, and to consider the relationship between the two heads of liability.

The Court stressed that whilst liability for nuisance has generally been regarded as strict, at least in the case of a Defendant who had been responsible for the creation of a nuisance, imposition of that liability had been kept in check by the principle of reasonable user. If the user is reasonable, the Defendant will not be liable. If the user is not reasonable, the Defendant will be liable, even though he may have exercised reasonable skill and care to avoid it. However, it did not follow that the Defendant should be held liable for damage which he could not reasonably foresee. In the Court's opinion developments in the law of negligence in the past 60 years pointed strongly towards a requirement that foreseeability should be a prerequisite of liability in damages for nuisance. In reaching this conclusion the Court referred to the *Wagon Mound* case (1961).

The Court then considered whether there was a similar prerequisite for recovery of damages under the rule in *Rylands* v *Fletcher*. The Court referred to the ratio in this case and concluded that the general tenor of the statement was that "knowledge, or at least foreseeability of the risk, is a prerequisite of the recovery of damages under the principle; but that the principle is one of strict liability in the sense that the Defendant may be held liable notwithstanding that he exercised all due care to prevent the escape from occurring" (per Lord Goff).

Thus, the Court took the view that foreseeability of damage should be regarded as a prerequisite of liability in damages under the *Rylands* v *Fletcher* rule, but if the damage was foreseeable the liability would be strict. The Appeal was allowed, since those responsible at Eastern Counties could not at the relevant time reasonably have foreseen that the damage in question might occur, and the claim of the Water Company for damages under the rule in *Rylands* v *Fletcher* failed.

The Court was of the opinion that as a general rule, it is more appropriate for strict liability in respect of operations of high risk to be imposed by Parliament than by the courts. That was of particular relevance in the case of environmental pollution regarding which public bodies, both national and international, were taking steps towards establishing legislation to promote the further protection of the environment.

In addition, the Court pointed out that in cases of historic pollution such as this it was not envisaged that statutory liability should be imposed. It would therefore be strange if liability for such pollution were to arise under a principle of common law. At the time of this judgment the Remediation Notice provisions of the 1994 Environment Bill were unforeseen (and probably not "reasonably foreseeable").

The Court also addressed the question of "natural use of land" and concluded that the storage of chemicals in substantial quantities and their use in the manner employed at Eastern counties premises could not fall within this exception. The mere fact that the use was common in the tanning industry which created employment in the area was insufficient to bring the use within the exception.

Future actions are likely to turn upon the question of foreseeability and the state of a Defendant's knowledge. As environmental regulations become stricter and awareness of environmental factors grows within industry, the class of potential Defendants who could claim lack of foreseeability or ignorance of risk will diminish substantially.

The likelihood of further civil claims may also increase due to the recent overturning of the decision of *Gillingham Borough Council* v *Chatham Dock Company* (1992) which dealt with the relationship between common law nuisance and activities for which specific planning permission has been granted.

Relationship between Common Law Nuisance and Planning Permission

It is well established that a Defendant in a nuisance action will have a good defence if he can demonstrate that his actions are authorised expressly by statute:

"It is now well settled that when Parliament by an express direction or by the necessary implication has authorised the construction and use of an undertaking or works, that carries with it an authority to do what is authorised with immunity from any action based on nuisance. The right of action is taken away; ...to this there is made a qualification, or condition, that the statutory powers are exercised without "negligence" – that word here being used in a special sense so as to require the undertaker, as a condition of obtaining immunity from action, to carry out other work and conduct of the operation with all reasonable regard and care for the interests of other persons..." (per Lord Wilberforce, *Allen* v *Gulf Oil Refinery Limited* (1981)).

This principle arose in the case of *Gillingham Borough Council* v *Medway (Chatham) Dock Company Limited* (1992). This case concerned the former Royal Naval Dockyard at Chatham which had been re-developed as a commercial port pursuant to planning permission granted by Gillingham Borough Council. The Council had been aware that the new use would give rise to HGV traffic but, at the request of the developers, had imposed no conditions limiting hours of operation. When the port became fully operational local residents complained about the noise and pollution caused by the commercial traffic.

Whilst the decision turned in part upon issues of estoppel, Buckley J's judgment was largely based upon the effect of the planning permission upon the nuisance action. In short, he held that the grant of planning permission rendered the activity immune from nuisance action.

This general principle, and Buckley J's specific decision, fell to be considered by the Court of Appeal in the recent case of *Wheeler* v *J J Saunders Limited* (1995). In that case the Court held that grants of planning permission for the intensification of an existing pig farming use did not render the farmer immune from liability in nuisance in respect of smells inevitably arising from that intensification. The *Gillingham* case could be distinguished on the basis that the grant of planning permission had the effect of changing the character of the neighbourhood. In *Wheeler* this was not the case. The Court rejected the proposition that any planning decision authorised any nuisance which must inevitably flow from it. Where major development altered the character of a neighbourhood with wide consequential effects a balancing exercise had to be carried out with the competing public and private interests prior to planning permission being granted. In such a case, the public interest had to be allowed to prevail and it would be inappropriate to grant an injunction (per Peter Gibson LJ). However, that was not the case in *Wheeler* and the planning permission did not prevent the Plaintiffs succeeding in their nuisance claim. The courts would be slow to extinguish private rights without compensation as a result of administrative decisions.

CHAPTER 6

Land Use Planning and Hazardous Substances

Key Points

- Traditionally inappropriate for dealing with pollution incidents and their consequences
- Need to check if extant planning conditions, agreements or obligations address emissions and operation of potentially polluting processes
- Hazardous Substances controls still largely untested in the courts

It is rare for a pollution incident to give rise to criminal or clean-up liability under the Town and Country Planning Acts. Historically, the Planning Acts have been aimed at regulating the general character of land use. Most activities which give rise to potential environmental liability are either authorised specifically under the terms of the Planning Acts or are lawful by reason of long use. A local planning authority can only instigate enforcement action under the Town and Country Planning Act 1990 if a breach of planning control has occurred. Breach of planning control is defined as carrying out development without the required planning permission or failing to comply with any condition or limitation subject to which permission has been granted (section 171A). It is important to note that no action can be taken in respect of anticipated breaches of control and action can only be taken by the local planning authority. No rights are granted to the private citizen and planning authorities have a discretion in determining whether or not to initiate enforcement action. This discretion must be exercised in a reasonable fashion and any authority exercising or failing to exercise its priority in an unreasonable manner may be subject to judicial review proceedings.

The term "development" is defined as the carrying out of building, engineering, mining or other operations in, on, over or under land or the making of any material change of use of any buildings or other land (section 55(1)). These terms are further defined in the Act. The definition of development and the general land use nature of planning law makes it by and large an inappropriate method to try and enforce liability in respect of pollution incidents. As discussed in Chapter 5 the existence of a specific planning permission can be a bar to a common law tortious action in respect of an environmental incident.

That being said there will be incidents where particular emission or, say, noise levels are such that specific conditions attached to planning permissions are breached. Similarly, (whilst this is rare) if an authorised use intensifies to an extreme degree the planning authority may be justified in determining that a material change of use has occurred. Similarly, any planning agreement under section 106 of the Act or its predecessor provisions may contain covenants limiting emissions or imposing other environmental controls.

Should a breach of planning control have occurred the planning authority will be empowered to issue the following notices:

Enforcement Notices
(Section 172 et seq*)*

Such a notice must specify:

- the matters which appear to the local planning authority to constitute the breach of planning control;
- the steps which the authority require to be taken or the activities which the authority require to cease;
- the date upon which it is to take effect;
- the period in which the required steps are to be taken.

A copy of the notice must be served on the owner and occupier of the land to which it relates and on any other person having an interest in the land, being an interest which in the opinion of the authority is materially affected by the notice. This definition is usually taken to include mortgagees. There must be a minimum 28 day period between service and the date specified as a date upon which the notice is to take effect. An appeal against the notice may be lodged at any time before the notice takes effect. An appeal to the Secretary of State has the effect of suspending operation of the notice pending determination of the appeal.

Once a notice takes effect non-compliance with its terms can give rise to criminal and/or clean-up liability. Where any steps required by the notice are not taken within the period for compliance the local planning authority may enter the land and take those steps and recover its reasonable expenses from the person who is then the owner of the land (section 178). Additionally, where those steps are not taken within the required period the person who is then the owner of the land is in breach of the notice and guilty of an offence (section 179(1) and (2)). In criminal proceedings it is a defence for the owner to show that he did everything he could be expected to do to secure compliance with the notice. Any person other than the owner of the land who has control of or an interest in the land is prohibited from carrying on any activity which is required by the notice to cease (section 179(4)). A defence is available to either of the above charges if the defendant was not served with a copy of the enforcement notice and the notice was not properly registered as required by the Act (section 179(7)).

Offences are triable either way and on summary conviction are punishable by a maximum £20,000 fine. Upon conviction on indictment the potential fine is unlimited. In determining the amount of any fine the Court must have particular regard to any financial benefit which has accrued or appears likely to accrue to the defendant in consequence of the offence (section 179(8)). The term "owner" is defined as a person, other than a mortgagee not in possession, who, whether in his own right or as trustee for any other person, is entitled to receive the rack rent of the land, or where the land is not let at a rack rent, any person who would be so entitled if it were so let (section 336). This definition includes mortgagees in possession and is wide enough to include receivers.

Where an offence is committed by a body corporate and is proved to have been committed with the consent or connivance of or to be attributable to the neglect of a director, manager, secretary or other similar officer or any person purporting to act as such that person is guilty of an offence as well as the body corporate (section 331).

Stop Notices
(Section 183 et seq)

As noted above the effectiveness of enforcement notices is severely limited by the fact that where an appeal is made to the Secretary of State the notice is ineffective pending determination of that appeal. If the local planning authority considers it expedient that an unauthorised activity should cease, notwithstanding the fact that an appeal either has been made or may be made at any time before the notice takes effect they may, when they serve the copy of the enforcement notice or at any time pending expiry of the period for compliance, serve a further notice, "a stop notice", prohibiting that activity.

A stop notice cannot be served:

- where the enforcement notice has taken effect;
- to prohibit the use of any building as a dwelling house or in respect of any activity which has been carried on (continuously or not) for a period of more than four years ending with service of the notice.

In practice stop notices are rarely served by local planning authorities as a successful appeal against the "parent" enforcement notice may give rise to a claim for compensation (section 186).

Breach of Condition Notices
(Section 187A)

Where planning permission is granted subject to conditions and any of those conditions are not complied with, the local planning authority may serve a "breach of condition notice" on any person carrying out the development or any person having control of the land, requiring him to secure compliance. If at the end of the period allowed for compliance with the notice (a minimum of 28 days) any of the conditions specified are still not complied with and the steps specified in the notice have not been taken or the activities specified not ceased, the person responsible is in breach of the notice and guilty of an offence. It is a defence for a person charged to prove that he took all reasonable measures to secure compliance or, as the case may be, that he no longer had control of the land. Offences are purely summary and punishable by a maximum fine of level 3 on the standard scale.

There is no provision contained in the Act for appeal to the Secretary of State or any other person or body in respect of a breach of condition notice. Accordingly, such notices may be a more effective remedy than an enforcement notice albeit that the potential penalties are less.

Injunctions

Specific power to apply for an injunction is given to local planning authorities by section 187B. Injunctions may be applied for in respect of actual or apprehended breaches of planning control.

Enforcement of Planning Obligations
(Section 106)

A planning obligation (whether unilateral or consensual) is specifically enforceable by injunction (section 106(5)). Additionally, where there is a breach of requirement in an obligation requiring the carrying out of operations, the authority may enter the land in question and recover their reasonable expenses from any person against whom the obligation is enforceable. Any person wilfully obstructing the exercise of this power is guilty of a summary offence punishable by a fine not exceeding level 3 on the standard scale (section 106(8)).

Hazardous Substances

Because of the problems of enforcing environmental standards through general planning legislation the Planning (Hazardous Substances) Act 1990 was introduced to give local authorities power to deal with the storage of hazardous chemicals. The chemicals in question are listed in the Planning (Hazardous Substances) Regulations 1992 (see Appendix 3). Against each chemical is listed a quantity ("the controlled quantity"). The presence of the controlled quantity, or any greater quantity, of a prescribed substance on land acts as a trigger for the requirement to obtain consent.

Criminal liability will arise if there is a breach of hazardous substances control (see section 23 Planning (Hazardous Substances) Act 1990). Breach of hazardous substances control is defined as having an amount of hazardous substance present on land equal to or exceeding the controlled quantity and either having no hazardous substances consent, or if there is hazardous substances consent in place where the quantity present exceeds that permitted, or alternatively breaching a condition attached to the hazardous substances consent.

Penalties for Non-Compliance

Breach of hazardous substances control is a criminal offence triable either way. The maximum penalty in the Magistrates Court is a £20,000 fine. In the Crown Court the maximum fine is unlimited. In determining the level of any penalty the court must have regard to any financial benefit which has accrued or appears likely to accrue to the defendant. Offences are committed by "the appropriate person". This will be the person in control of the land although in some circumstances the definition of appropriate persons is also extended to others such as persons who knowingly cause or allow a substance to be present.

"The person in control" is not defined in the Act and as yet there is no body of case law on this legislation. However, the term will include occupational tenants and most probably excludes landlords. Almost certainly it will include mortgagees in possession and receivers. Statutory defences including the standard one that the defendant took all reasonable precautions and exercised all due diligence to avoid commission of the offence are available.

As well there being direct criminal liability for breach of hazardous substances control, authorities also have the power to serve hazardous substances contravention notices which are very much akin to planning enforcement notices. Accordingly further criminal liability may arise for breach of a notice and clean up powers may become exercisable by authorities. Authorities have specific powers to apply for injunctions in respect of actual or apprehended breaches of control.

Hazardous Substances Consents

Applications for consent should be made to the Hazardous Substances Authority ("HSA"). The HSA will usually be the district or London borough council. However, the HSA will be the county council where the land is question is in a non-metropolitan county and is either situated in a National Park or used for mineral working or (in England) used for waste disposal. However, if the land is in a National Park for which a joint or special planning board is constituted that board will be the HSA. In the Broads the HSA will be the Broads Authority (unless the above provisions relating to county councils and joint or special planning boards apply) and if the land is within the area of an urban development corporation that corporation will be the HSA. If the land is within an area of a housing action trust which is vested with the powers of the local planning authority that trust will be the HSA. See section 3 of the Act.

An application for consent should be made to the HSA where a quantity of a prescribed hazardous substance equal to or exceeding the controlled quantity is to be present on land. No consent is necessary where the quantity of the substance in question is less than the controlled quantity. The Act contains no definition of what area of land an application should relate to. Neither is this question addressed in any accompanying guidance. However, it should be noted that in determining whether or not the controlled quantity has been reached regard is had to other land and structures controlled by the same person within a 500 metre radius (see section 4(2)).

As mentioned above the penalties for non-compliance are aimed at persons in control of the land but this term remains undefined in the Act.

The 1992 Regulations set out the form, content and procedure for applications submitted to HSAs. In particular, provisions are made for consultation between HSA and various other bodies. It is safe to assume that an HSA will be most guided by the comments of the Health and Safety Executive. Accordingly, it would be wise for applicants to engage in pre-application consultations with the HSE in order to determine their likely requirements.

In granting any consent the HSA may impose conditions restricting how and where any substance is to be kept or used, the times between which such substances may be present and requirements of permanent removal upon or before specific dates. Additionally, the grant of consent may be conditional upon the commencement or partial or complete execution of development authorised by a specific planning permission. Conditions may only be imposed governing how a hazardous substance is to be kept or used if the authority has the support of the HSE (see section 10 of the Act). Applications may be made for lifting or varying conditions attached to consents. See section 13.

Revocation and Modification

HSAs have a general power to revoke or modify consents if they consider it "expedient". Specific revocation powers are also granted:

- where there has been a material change of use of the land to which the consent relates;
- where planning permission has been granted and commenced for development which would involve a material change of use;
- where the substance or substances to which the consent relate have not been present upon the land for at least five years.

An order revoking a consent does not take effect unless and until it is confirmed by the Secretary of State: see sections 14 and 15. Compensation is payable to persons suffering damage in consequence of such an order, in consequence of a depreciation in the value of his interest in the land in question or minerals in on or under it or in consequence of his enjoyment of such land or minerals being disturbed. See section 16.

A hazardous substances consent is automatically revoked where there is a change in the person in control of part of the land to which it relates unless an application for its continuation has previously been submitted. Where such an application is made the HSA may modify the consent or revoke it. Compensation may be payable as a result of such revocation or modification. See sections 17, 18 and 19.

As with matters of planning control, decisions of HSAs may be appealed to the Secretary of State and from him to the High Court. See sections 21 and 22.

CHAPTER 7

Wildlife and Habitat Protection and other Ecological Controls

Key Points

- Complex series of criminal sanctions aimed at protecting extensive lists of species referred to in the 1981 Act
- Similarly extensive provisions laying down defences and exceptions to basic protections
- SSSI designation essentially a mechanism to delay operations
- Important new Regulations implementing EC Habitats Directive

The principal legislation dealing with wildlife conservation is contained in Part I of the Wildlife and Countryside Act 1981. Schedules 1 to 10 of the Act set out in detail the species of birds, animals and plants to which the various degrees of protection apply.

Wild and Captive Birds

Sections 1 to 8 set out the various criminal provisions for protection of wild birds, their nests and eggs, the sale of live or dead wild birds or eggs, the registration of certain captive birds and the conditions under which any captive birds (except poultry) should be kept.

Section 1 creates the following offences:

- to intentionally kill, injure or take any wild bird
- to intentionally take, damage or destroy the nest of any wild bird whilst it is in use or being built; and
- to intentionally take or destroy an egg of any wild bird (sub-section (1)).

WILDLIFE PROTECTION

In addition to these "intentional" offences, any person who has in his possession or control:

- any live or dead wild bird or any part of it or anything derived from such a bird; or
- an egg of a wild bird or any part of such an egg

is guilty of an offence (sub-section (2)). It is a defence to a charge under sub-section (2) if the Defendant can show that the bird or egg has not been killed, taken or sold illegally. These offences apply to all wild birds but if the bird in question in listed in Schedule 1, special penalties apply to persons convicted. That is to say the usual maximum fine of £200 is increased to £1,000. Furthermore, any person who intentionally disturbs a wild bird included in Schedule 1 whilst building its nest or is in, on or near a nest containing eggs or young or disturbs the dependent young of such a bird, is guilty of such an offence and liable to such a special penalty (section 1 (5)).

Section 2 specifies exceptions for the killing or taking of particular birds outside defined "close seasons". Section 3 empowers the Secretary of State to make Orders designating "areas of special protection" and prescribing additional criminal offences applicable to such areas. That is to say, in effect, to designate sanctuaries either for all wild birds or for designated birds. Additional defences are laid down in section 4.

Certain methods of killing or taking wild birds are prohibited by section 5. In particular, spring traps, gins, snares, hooks and lines and electrical devices and the use of poisonous, poisoned or stupefying substances, nets, baited boards, bird-lime or similar substances and the use of:

- bows and crossbows;
- explosives;
- automatic or semi-automatic weapons;
- shotguns with internal muzzle diameters of more than $1^1/4''$;
- night sights;
- artificial lightning, mirrors or other dazzling devices;
- gas or smoke, and
- chemical wetting agents.

Additionally, the use of sound recordings or any tethered live birds or animals or blind, maimed or injured animals as decoys is prohibited as is the use of mechanically propelled vehicles for pursuit purposes. The Secretary of State has power to amend the above list generally or in relation to specific kinds of wild bird but this power is only exercisable in compliance with an international obligation in relation to the use of firearms for killing or taking wild birds.

It is a defence to proceedings relating to the setting of traps etc. if the act was done in the interests of public health, agriculture, forestry, fisheries or nature conservation in relation to wild animals that can lawfully be killed or taken and that the Defendant took all reasonable precautions to prevent injury to wild birds (section 5(4A)). Additional defences relating to cage traps, the use of nets in a duck decoy or the use of cage traps are provided for in sub-section (5).

Section 6 places restrictions upon the sale or offer or exposure for sale of live or dead wild birds or their eggs and similarly the publication of advertisements relating to such matters also amounts to a criminal offence.

Section 7 and Schedule 4 make provision for the registration and ringing of specific species if kept in captivity. Section 8 contains a more general prohibition against the keeping or confining of any birds in cages or other receptacles which are not sufficient in height, length or breadth to permit the bird to stretch its wings freely. This general prohibition does not apply to poultry or to birds in the course of conveyance, being shown at exhibitions or competitions (provided the confinement does not in aggregate exceed 72 hours) or to a wild bird undergoing examination or treatment by a Vet. Section 8(3) lays down an offence of engaging in events involving the liberation of captive birds for the purpose of being shot immediately after their liberation.

Protection of other Animals

Section 9 creates the following offences aimed at protecting the species listed in Schedule 5. Subject to specific exceptions, it is an offence:

- to kill, injure or take any protected animal;
- to have in your possession or control any live or dead protected animal (including any part of such animal or anything derived therefrom);
- intentionally to damage or destroy or obstruct access to any structure or place used by a protected animal for shelter or protection or to intentionally damage or destroy or obstruct access to any structure or place used by a protected animal for shelter or

protection or to intentionally disturb any such animal while it is occupying such a structure or place;

- to sell, offer or expose for sale or have in your possession or transport for the purpose of sale any live or dead protected animal (including parts of such animals or anything derived therefrom) or to publish or cause to be published any advertisement likely to be understood as conveying dealing in such things (section 9(5)).

Section 10 lays down defences including actions required by the Ministry of Agriculture or certain requirements of the Animal Health Act 1981.

Other general defences under section 10 apply:

- where the animal has been disabled otherwise than by the Defendant's unlawful act and was taken solely for the purpose of tending and releasing the animal when no longer disabled;
- with regard to killing the protected animal where it had been seriously disabled otherwise than by the Defendant's act and there was no reasonable chance of its recovery; and
- where the Defendant's act was the incidental result of a lawful operation and could not reasonably have been avoided.

Other specific defences and limitations are provided for in sections 9 and 10.

Certain mammals have specific statutes setting out specific protections such as the Ground Game Act 1880, the Dogs (Protection of Livestock) Act 1953, the Deer Act 1963, the Conservation of Seals Act 1970 and the Badgers Act 1992.

Protection of Wild Plants

Section 13 sets out protections for the species of wild plants listed in Schedule 8. It is an offence:

- intentionally to pick, uproot or destroy such wild plants;
- to sell, offer or expose for sale or have in your possession or transport for the purpose of sale any live or dead protected wild plant or any part thereof or anything deriving from such a plant;
- to publish or cause to be published an advertisement likely to be understood as conveying dealing in such things.

Persons charged will have defence if they can show the act was an incidental result of a lawful operation and could not have reasonably been avoided.

Sites of Special Scientific Interest

Where English Nature are of the opinion that any area of land is of special interest by reason of its flora, fauna or geological or physiographical features it is under a duty to notify that fact to:

- the local planning authority;
- every owner and occupier of that land; and
- the Secretary of State (section 28 Wildlife and Countryside Act 1981).

Persons notified are given a period of at least three months in which to make representations which English Nature are under a duty to consider. The notification details must specify the flora, fauna, physiological or geological feature which English Nature believe to be of special interest and any operations which appear to them to be likely to damage that flora, fauna or those features.

English Nature have a period of nine months beginning with the date on which notification was served on the Secretary of State to withdraw the notification or to confirm it (with or without modifications).

The owners and occupiers of land affected by such a notification are prohibited from carrying out or causing or permitting the carrying out of the operations specified in the notification unless prior written notice of a proposal has been given to English Nature specifying the nature of the operation and the land upon which it is to be carried out and:

- the operation is carried out in accordance with English Nature's consent;
- the operation is carried out in accordance with the terms of an agreement under section 16 of the National Parks and Access to the Countryside Act 1949 or section 15 of the Countryside Act 1968; or
- four months have expired from the giving of notice.

The four month period may be shortened by agreement (sub-sections (6A) and (6B)).

A person who carries out prohibited operations in an SSSI without English Nature's consent or in accordance with an agreement, is liable on summary conviction to a fine not exceeding level 4 on the standard scale unless the operation is carried out with "reasonable excuse". It is a reasonable excuse if the operation was an emergency operation, particulars of which are notified to English Nature as soon as practicable after commencement of the operation. Also it is a reasonable excuse if the operation was authorised by specific planning permission granted on an application made under the Planning Act (i.e. as opposed to permission granted by a Development Order). Where planning applications are submitted which affect an SSSI, the local planning authority is under a duty to consult English Nature.

Where the Secretary of State believes that an SSSI is of particular interest he may, after consultation with English Nature, make a Nature Conservation Order. Such Orders enable English Nature to prevent the carrying out of specified operations even after expiry of the four month notification period referred to above and also to acquire the land in question either by agreement or compulsorily (section 29).

Conservation (Natural Habitats etc) Regulations 1994 and Habitats Directive

These Regulations came into force on 30 October 1994 and implement the EC Habitats Directive. The Secretary of State for the Environment and the Minister of Agriculture, Fisheries and Food and the Nature Conservancy Council are required to exercise their functions so as to secure compliance with the Directive. The Directive requires the designation of Special Areas of Conservation (SAC's) for certain habitat types and species which are rare or endangered at Community level and aims to contribute to the maintenance of biodiversity by establishing a network of SAC's. Member States have until June 1995 to submit a draft national list of sites of Community importance to the Commission. A definitive list of sites is to be agreed with the Commission by 1998 and all these sites are to be designated by 2004. In the 1994 Regulations, the sites are referred to as "European sites". Regulations 16 and 17 make provision for management agreements for the site and Regulations 18 to 27 make provision for the control of damaging operations. Regulations 28 to 32 make provision for Bye-laws and Compulsory Purchase Orders.

Regulation 39 makes it an offence, subject to certain exceptions, deliberately to capture, kill or disturb certain wild animals or to trade in them and Regulation 43 makes it an offence, subject to exceptions, to pick, collect, cut, uproot or destroy those plants or trade in them.

In town and country planning terms the effect of proposed development on a European site is to be considered before a grant of planning permission can be issued. Subject to certain exceptions the grant of permission is restricted where the integrity of the site would be adversely affected. Planning permissions granted before the date on which a site becomes a European site is to be reviewed and in certain circumstances revoked where the integrity of the site would be adversely affected. Planning Policy Guide Note 9 gives guidance to local planning authorities in the exercise of their functions in this respect.

Tree Preservation Orders

A local planning authority may make a Tree Preservation Order to preserve individual trees, groups of trees or woodlands if it appears that "it is expedient in the interests of the amenity" (section 198 (1) of the TCPA 1990). A TPO may prohibit (subject to exemptions specified in the order) the lopping, topping, felling, uprooting, wilful damage or destruction of trees and an Order may also provide for the replanting of woodland areas felled in the course of permitted forestry operations, The protection afforded by a TPO is not absolute. It is open to a person wishing to lop, top, fell or uproot etc to apply to the Local Planning Authority for consent.

The procedure for applying for consent is very similar to the procedure for planning applications. However, the usual planning procedures relating to publicising applications and notifying owners and tenants does not apply. A TPO may be made to apply to trees to be planted where that planting is required by a planning condition. However a TPO cannot apply to a tree which is dead, dying or dangerous nor to works carried out on a tree in compliance with a statutory obligation or so far as is necessary to prevent or abate a nuisance.

When considering whether or not it is necessary to apply to the Planning Authority for consent to fell or carry out works or consider whether or not an offence has been committed, it is important to look at the original order itself. When a local planning authority makes an Order it is necessary for it to be in the form (or substantially in the form) set out in regulations (the Town & Country Planning (Tree Preservation Order) Regulations 1969). However it should be noted that the prescribed form has evolved significantly over the years. Accordingly, a Tree Preservation Order made today will differ significantly from an Order made, say, 20 or 30 years' ago.

The Order will lay down a series of exemptions, the most important being that Orders do not apply where felling of or works to a tree are immediately required in order to carry out development for which planning permission has been applied for and granted.

Contravention of a TPO is a criminal offence triable either way. The maximum penalty on summary conviction is a fine not exceeding £20,000. On indictment the maximum penalty is an unlimited fine. In determining the amount of any fine the court must have particular regard to any financial benefit which has accrued or appears likely to accrue to the Defendant in consequence of the offence (section 210 TCPA 1990).

If a protected tree is removed, uprooted or destroyed in contravention of an Order, it is the duty of the owner of the land to plant another tree of an appropriate size and species at the same place as soon as he reasonably can. If he fails to do so, the local planning authority can serve notice requiring compliance. Appeals against such notices lie to the Secretary of State. However, once such a notice becomes effective, the local planning authority may enter the land, plant the replacement tree or trees and recover from the owner their reasonable expenses. These expenses will also be a Local Land Charge (section 209(5) and the Town and Country Planning General Regulations 1992). Both the High Court and the County Court have jurisdiction to grant injunctions at the behest of a local planning authority in support of a Tree Preservation Order (*Newport Borough Council* v *Khan, Khan and Roderick* (1990)).

Trees in Conservation Areas

Subject to exceptions prescribed by the Secretary of State, trees within Conservation Areas benefit from a similar form of protection to that provided by TPO's. It is an offence to fell, top, lop, uproot, wilfully damage or destroy any non-TPO protected tree within a Conservation Area (section 211). It is a defence for a person charged to prove that he served notice of his intention to carry out the works in question on the local planning authority and those works were carried out with their consent or after the expiry of six weeks from the date of that notice (but before the expiry of two years from that date). This six week period is designed to give the local planning authority the opportunity to make a TPO if it so wishes. Provision is made for the replacement of trees removed in breach of these provisions analogous to the provisions relating to TPO protected trees above (see section 213).

The Town and Country Planning (Tree Preservation Order) (Amendment) (Trees in Conservation Areas) (Excepted Cases) Regulations 1975 disapplies these provisions in the case of:

- felling, uprooting, topping or lopping of trees which are dead, dying or dangerous or where works are required to comply with a statutory obligation or to abate a nuisance; or
- works are required pursuant to Forestry Dedication Covenants, Forestry Commission operations, at the request of specific public bodies, immediately required for development for which planning permission is granted and fruit trees; and
- felling in accordance with a Felling Licence granted by the Forestry Commission
- felling, uprooting, topping or lopping of a tree on land occupied by a local planning authority and with their consent;
- trees with a diameter of 75mm or less or 100mm or less where the works are needed to improve the growth of other trees. The diameter is measured over the bark at a point 1.5m above ground level.

Policy Advice upon Tree Preservation issues is contained in Department of the Environment Circular 36/78.

CHAPTER 8

Minimising Risk in Property and Corporate Transactions

Key Points

- Importance of information gathering exercise and Environmental Information Regulations 1992
- Need to work with other disciplines
- Importance of Environmental Audit
- Risk allocation essentially a function of price and bargaining strength

In all corporate and property transactions it is traditional for a great deal of time and effort (and client's money) to be expended in identifying the risks arising from or attached to the site or business in question and allocating them between the parties. It is not surprising that given the upsurge in interest in environmental issues that corporate and, more particularly, property lawyers and their clients have turned their attention to environmental risks. In many respects the approach adopted towards dealing with environmental risks is no different from dealing with any other risk. That is to say the question of warranties and indemnities will arise almost as a matter of inevitability.

It is not the aim of this chapter to examine the normal concepts of corporate and property transactional practice but rather to focus upon what effect environmental questions will have upon the usual considerations. Before the pros and cons of the various mechanisms are considered, it is as well to bear in mind the following:

- Before the parties can debate issues of risk minimisation and allocation it is necessary to identify and quantify those risks as far as possible. In practice, this will involve the client instructing specialist consultants to carry out an environmental audit. It should be borne in mind that whilst lawyers may not be the best people to advise upon the scientific minutiae of a consultant's report, it is advisable to assist the client in drafting a suitable specification for the consultant, drawing up a suitable shortlist of consultants and assessing their standard terms of engagement and professional indemnity cover. Consideration should be given to an auditor being instructed through a solicitor with a view to the audit report benefiting from legal privilege (a point yet to be tested by the UK courts).

● The perennial question of whether or not a transaction proceeds by way of asset purchase or share purchase needs to be considered in the light of the potential environmental liabilities. As will be noted from the preceding chapters, there is no uniformity between the various statutory regimes as to who is liable in the event of a breach of control. That is to say in the case of a process governed by the IPC regime, criminal liability attaches to the person carrying out the process. A "share" purchaser will stand in the shoes of the vendor-operator and be liable for any extant breaches. Similarly, if there is a risk that controlled waters may have been polluted contrary to the Water Resources Act, liability attaches to the person causing the pollution as opposed to "owners" or "occupiers". These factors may weigh heavily in the balance in favour of proceeding by way of an asset purchase. An assessment has to be made as to what activities have been carried upon the site in question and which of the various statutory regimes may have been breached.

The parties to a transaction involving the sale of a company or property may allocate the risk of any potential liabilities between them as they see fit. Traditionally, warranties and indemnities have been employed for this purpose. It is not surprising then that a growing awareness of the emerging significance of environmental liabilities has been accompanied by interest in the use and form of these mechanisms.

A warranty, being a contractual promise that a particular state of affairs exists, should make explicit any assumptions made by the purchaser regarding the property or business in question. It should be specific, precise and objective. Warranties need to elicit information and to allocate liability. They are a reflection of the value (or at least price) of a transaction and the bargaining strength of the parties. Breach of the warranty gives rise to a contractual right to damages. Indemnities are simply a promise by one party to reimburse the other for any loss suffered upon the happening of a particular event. There is no need to prove or to mitigate loss and, unsurprisingly, are rare in practice. It is worthwhile to note that the new contaminated land provisions in the current Environment Bill refer to the possible "transfer" of liability between contracting parties. Neither of the traditional mechanisms operates to transfer primary liability but rather to apportion expense in the event of liability arising against one or other party.

The alternatives available to the parties can be summarised as follows:

- use standard warranties which are then tailored to the particular transaction;
- rely upon a "Phase I" or "desk top" audit coupled with a general condition that the vendor is not knowingly in breach of any provision, together with indemnities to cover any specific problems that are identified;
- a rigorous audit on the basis of which the purchaser chooses whether to accept the risks or to negotiate a reduction in price.

The Property Transaction

In the property context, the overriding principle governing relations between the parties remains "caveat emptor". The inclusion of warranties in the contract of sale will rarely be a vendor's preferred option. Instead the purchaser is likely to be asked in the first instance to rely on its own investigations. Reference will normally be made to searches, preliminary enquiries made of the vendor's solicitors and perhaps a "Phase I" type audit, consisting of a site visit, detailed investigation of compliance with regulatory authorities and a surface examination of the site. Investigations of this kind are becoming a more normal part of the property transaction.

The sources of information to which the purchaser will have access for the purposes of identifying contamination are quite extensive. There are, in the first instance, a number of public registers of information held by planning, health and safety and pollution control authorities. A great deal of information is available through Local Authority Searches and the standard "Con 29" Enquiries. They contain details of planning consents, hazardous substances matters, enforcement action etc. Other environmental information may also be the subject of enquiries of public bodies pursuant to the Environmental Information Regulations 1992.

The Corporate Transaction

Warranties and indemnities are more likely to arise in a corporate transaction.

Standard warranties will deal with regulatory compliance, the absence of actual or contingent liability as well as the absence of litigation and material enforcement orders, notices etc.. A warranty as to the absence of any hazardous substances on the property may also be sought. Again, warranties of this kind will be agreed against the background of information provided by the vendor company in respect to the purchaser's environmental requisitions and a "Phase I" audit.

The principal subject of negotiation relating to warranties will usually revolve around the kinds of limitations by which the vendor will seek to protect itself and which the purchaser is willing to accept. Typically, a warranty will be limited to a two or three year period which gives the purchaser time to carry out further audits and compare the results with its pre-contract audit thereby identifying any emerging problems. Whilst a purchaser may seek warranties which are not limited in time these are rarely, if ever, given.

Financial limitations may also be imposed, often limited by reference to the consideration paid. Again, a purchaser may seek an amendment to this limitation according to the subject and the information at hand. Finally, warranties may be limited by reference to the factual knowledge of the party giving the warranty, particularly where the purchaser has already made its own investigations. Formulae such as "To the best of the warrantor's knowledge" or "So far as the warrantor is aware" are not uncommon.

Drafting and negotiating warranties and indemnities can be a problematic and lengthy process. Enforcing them can be even more so. It should be borne in mind that a quicker, cheaper and more certain transaction may result if the parties take a view on environmental risk, as they may with any other risk and simply negotiate an adjustment to the purchase price.

So far as current drafting practice with respect to warranties is concerned, a number of points arise. Terms such as "hazardous substances", "pollution", "damage", "harm", "environment" and even "environmental law" require clear definition.

Consideration should also be given to alternative mechanisms for allocating and limiting liability. These include:

- "ringfencing" potentially polluting or polluted sites or parts of sites ("assets" which may turn out to be liabilities dragging down the value of the rest of the property or company) so that they are not included in the transaction or are transferred to a separate "vehicle";
- the retention of part of the purchase monies in an escrow account which might then be applied towards any problems that emerge after the agreement has been concluded;
- the use of a conditional contract, the agreement made subject to a satisfactory audit; or
- a provision for post-completion investigations and an agreement on the allocation of any clean- up costs which appear at this stage.

Lenders

Lenders are becoming increasingly aware of the need to minimise their own risks which arise when lending on environmentally sensitive projects. The concerns of lenders arising out of environmental law are threefold:

(i) they wish to be reassured about the future viability of the borrower's business;

(ii) they are concerned about the impact potential liabilities upon the value of their securities (eg in the event of clean-up costs being imposed or regulatory requirements having a detrimental impact upon the market) and, perhaps more importantly;

(iii) the possible risk of their own direct liability for environmental clean-up costs in the event of them enforcing their security.

Meeting the BATNEEC requirements of IPC may place an onerous burden upon the borrower. Similarly, adverse publicity arising from environmental issues may lead to loss of custom. We are already seeing major commercial buyers requiring their supplier to demonstrate "environmental friendliness". Additionally as mentioned in previous chapters the individual statutory regimes may include mortgagees in possession and receivers within their definitions of "owners" or "occupiers". Another area which is yet to be fully explored in this country is the extent to which lenders may be directly liable for environmental matters if found to be acting as shadow directors of their borrowers.

It is becoming common for lenders to protect themselves by looking at the environmental standing of borrowers, incorporating contractual provisions into the loan documentation and adopting credit approval procedures reflecting environmental concerns. For example, banks now consider:

- the current regulatory standing and compliance record of their customers,
- questions of potential liability for clean-up and remedial costs;
- projected costs of compliance with future regulatory developments.

It has become common for loan documentation to include:

- specific representations and warranties as to compliance,
- undertakings as to continuing compliance;
- indemnities against any loss that the lenders might suffer as a result of non compliance.

Events of default have been extended to include material breaches of environmental law and reporting and information covenants included.

Insurance

Traditionally, environmental risks in this country were covered by the usual public liability policies. It is only comparatively recently that insurers have started to exclude pollution liability from such policies except to the extent that it is caused by a sudden and accidental event. Perennially, the EU has considered making cover mandatory for certain operations. Whilst some insurers have considered the potential market, many who have ventured into it have ceased to offer cover. However a minority of insurers continue to offer environmental impairment liability policies. Such policies are available on a claims-made basis. That is to say the policies only cover claims actually made within the period of coverage as opposed to occurrence based policies where cover is given if the damage occurred within the period of cover even though claims may be made some time afterwards.

Environmental impairment policies are only given on a site specific basis requiring a site survey giving a detailed view of the risks, past history and risks of costs of clean-up. An environmental impairment survey would usually include a review of air emissions and liquid discharge performance levels against local and national limits, a survey of the processes involved to identify plant or procedural defects, an inspection of facilities for storage or potentially hazardous substances, a review of the potential insured's waste management policy and observations of on and off site transport movements to assess noise nuisance levels and spillage risks. Policies are offered for a limited time span and only renewed on the basis of a fresh site survey.

Conclusions

There remains some reluctance on the part of practitioners to spend a great deal of time negotiating environmental warranties and undertakings without the benefit of further judicial guidance regarding the nature and extent of the relevant liabilities, the meaning to be given to specific terms such as "contamination" and the significance to be attached to particular issues such as the foreseeability of risk. However, the magnitude risk is such that it is essential for clients to be advised of the various options available to them even if this results in the nature of a transaction altering in a fundamental manner or even not proceeding at all.

Whilst the American experience may not be directly comparable to this country it serves as a reminder, if one were needed, that potential litigants, with or without the encouragement of their lawyers, are never slow to spot a potential defendant. Those with the deepest pockets will usually find themselves identified as the favoured targets. Those with the most comprehensive insurance cover are ideal. Rightly or wrongly this will often narrow the field down to a client's own professional team in the event of him receiving an unwanted and unexpected clean up bill.

Appendix I

Timetable for Implementing Integrated Pollution Control

Process	Comes within IPC	Apply Between	Chief Inspector's Guidance Note Issues
Fuel & Power Industry			
Combustion (>50MWth)	01.04.91	01.04.91 & 30.04.91	01.04.91
Boilers & Furnaces			
Gasification	01.04.92	01.04.92 & 30.06.92	01.10.91
Carbonisation	01.04.92	01.04.92 & 30.06.92	01.10.91
Combustion (remainder)	01.04.92	01.04.92 & 30.06.92	01.10.91
Petroleum	01.04.92	01.04.92 & 30.06.92	01.10.91
Waste Disposal Industry			
Incineration	01.08.92	01.08.92 & 31.10.92	01.02.92
Chemical Recovery	01.08.92	01.08.92 & 31.10.92	01.02.92
Waste Derived Fuel	01.08.92	01.08.92 & 31.10.92	01.02.92
Chemical Industry			
Cement	01.12.92	01.12.92 & 28.02.93	01.06.92
Asbestos	01.12.92	01.12.92 & 28.02.93	01.06.92
Fibre	01.12.92	01.12.92 & 28.02.93	01.06.92
Glass	01.12.92	01.12.92 & 28.02.93	01.06.92
Ceramic	01.12.92	01.12.92 & 28.02.93	01.06.92

Process	Comes within IPC	Apply Between	Chief Inspector's Guidance Note Issues
Chemical Industry			
Petrochemical	01.05.93	01.05.93 & 31.07.93	01.11.92
Organic	01.05.93	01.05.93 & 31.07.93	01.11.92
Chemical Pesticide	01.05.93	01.05.93 & 31.07.93	01.11.92
Pharmaceutical	01.05.93	01.05.93 & 31.07.93	01.11.92
Acid Manufacturing	01.11.93	01.11.93 & 31.01.94	01.05.93
Halogen	01.11.93	01.11.93 & 31.01.94	01.05.93
Chemical Fertiliser	01.11.93	01.11.93 & 31.01.94	01.05.93
Bulk Chemical Storage	01.11.93	01.11.93 & 31.01.94	01.05.93
Inorganic Chemical	01.05.94	01.05.94 & 31.07.94	01.11.93
Metal Industry			
Iron and Steel	01.01.95	01.01.95 & 31.03.95	01.07.94
Smelting	01.01.95	01.01.95 & 31.03.95	01.09.94
Non-Ferrous	01.05.95	01.05.95 & 31.07.95	01.11.94
Other Industry			
Paper Manufacturing	01.11.95	01.11.95 & 31.01.96	01.05.95
Di-isocyanate	01.11.95	01.11.95 & 31.01.96	01.05.95
Tar and Bitumen	01.11.95	01.11.95 & 31.01.96	01.05.95
Uranium	01.11.95	01.11.95 & 31.01.96	01.05.95
Coating	01.11.95	01.11.95 & 31.01.96	01.05.95
Coating Manufacturing	01.11.95	01.11.95 & 31.01.96	01.05.95
Timber	01.11.95	01.11.95 & 31.01.96	01.05.95
Animal and Plant Treatment	01.11.95	01.11.95 & 31.01.96	01.05.95

Appendix 2

Processes Subject to Local Authority Air Emission Control

Combustion processes
Boilers and Furnaces, 20-50 MW Net Rates Thermal Input
Gas Turbines, 20-50 MW Net Rates Thermal Input
Compression Ignition Engines, 20-50 MW Net Rated Thermal Input
Waste Oil Burners, Less than 0.4 MW Net Rated Thermal Input
Waste Oil or Recovered Oil Burners, up to 3 MW Net Rated Thermal Input
Tyre and Rubber Combustion Processes between 0.4 and 3 MW Net Rated Thermal Input
Straw Combustion Processes between 0.4 and 3 MW Net Rated Thermal Input
Wood Combustion Processes between 0.4 and 3 MW Net Rated Thermal Input
Poultry Litter Combustion Processes between 0.4 and 3 MW Rated Thermal Input

Glass Processes
Glass (Excluding Lead Glass) Manufacturing Process
Lead Glass Manufacturing Process
Processes for the Polishing or Etching of Glass or Glass products using hydrofluoric acid

Ceramic Processes
Manufacture of Heavy Clay Goods and Refractory Goods

Incinerators
General Waste Incineration Processes under 1 Tonne per hour
Sewage Sludge Incineration Processes under 1 Tonne per hour
Clinical Waste Incineration Processes under 1 Tonne per hour
Animals Carcase Incineration Processes under 1 Tonne per hour
Crematoria

Timber Processes
Manufacture of Timber and Wood-based Products
Chemical Treatment of Timber and Wood-based Products
Processes for the Manufacture of Particleboard and Fibreboard

Maggot Breeding
Maggot Breeding Processes

Non-ferrous
Furnaces for the extraction of Non-Ferrous Metal from Scrap

Cement and Lime
Blending, Packing, Loading and use of Bulk Cement

Animal and Plant Treatment Processes
Fur Breeding Processes

Appendix 3

Hazardous Substances and Controlled Quantities

Part A: Toxic Substances

	Column 1 *Hazardous substances*	Column 2 *Controlled quantities*	
		(in *tonnes*, unless otherwise stated)	
1.	Acetone Cyanohydrin (2-Cyanopropan-2-ol)	200	
2.	Acrolein (2-Propenal)	200	
3.	Acrylonitrile	20	
4.	Allyl alcohol (2-Propen-1-ol)	200	
5.	Allylamine	200	
6.	Ammonia (anhydrous or as solution containing more than 50% by weight of ammonia)	100	
7.	Arsenic trioxide, Arsenious (III) acid and salts	1	
8.	Arsine (Arsenic hydride)	1	
9.	Bromine	40	
10.	Carbon disulphide	20	
11.	Chlorine	10	
12.	Ethylene dibromide (1.2-Dibromoethane)	50	
13.	Ethyeneimine	50	
14.	Formaldehyde (>90%)	50	
15.	Hydrogen chloride (liquefied gas)	250	
16.	Hydrogen cyanide	20	
17.	Hydrogen fluoride	10	
18.	Hydrogen selenide	1	
19.	Hydrogen sulphide	50	

Column 1 *Hazardous substances*		Column 2 *Controlled quantities*	
		(in *tonnes*, unless otherwise stated)	
20.	Methyl bromide (Bromoethane)	200	
21.	Methyl isocyanate	150	kilograms
22.	Nickel tetracarbonyl	1	
23.	Nitrogen oxides	50	
24.	Oxygen difluoride	1	
25.	Pentaborane	1	
26.	Phosgene	750	kilograms
27.	Phosphine (Hydrogen phosphide)	1	
28.	Propleneimine	50	
29.	Selenium hexafluoride	1	
30.	Stibine (Antimony hydride)	1	
31.	Sulphur dioxide	20	
32.	Sulphur trioxide (including the sulphur trioxide content in oleum)	15	
33.	Tellurium hexafluoride	1	
34.	2,3,7,8-Tetrachlorodibenzo-p-dioxin (TCDD)	1	kilogram
35.	Tetraethyl lead	50	
36.	Tetramethyl lead	50	

Part B: Highly Reactive Substances and Explosive Substances

Column 1 *Hazardous substances*	Column 2 *Controlled quantities*	
	(in *tonnes*, unless otherwise stated)	
37. Acetylene (Ethyne) when a gas subject to a pressure not exceeding 620 millibars above that of the atmosphere, and not otherwise deemed to be an explosive by virtue of Order in Council No 30[1] as amended by the Compressed Acetylene Order 1947[2], or when contained in a homogeneous porous substance in cylinders in accordance with Order of Secretary of State No 9[3], made under the Explosives Act 1875[4]	50	
38. Ammonium nitrate and mixtures containing ammonium nitrate where the nitrogen content derived from the ammonium nitrate exceeds 28% of the mixture by weight other than – (i) mixtures to which the Explosives Act 1875 applies: (ii) ammonium nitrate based products manufactured chemically for use as fertiliser which comply with Council Directive 80/876/EEC([5]); or (iii) compound fertilisers.	500	
39. Aqueous solutions containing more than 90 parts by weight of ammonium nitrate per 100 parts by weight of solution ammonium nitrate per 100 parts by weight of solution	500	

[1]S.R. & O. 1937/54
[2]S.R. & O. 1947/805
[3]S.R. & O. 1919/869

[4]1875 c.17
[5]OJ No L250, 23.9.80. p.7.

Column 1 Hazardous substances		Column 2 Controlled quantities
		(in *tonnes*, unless otherwise stated)
40.	Ammonium nitrate based products manufactured chemically for use as fertilisers which comply with Council Directive 80/876/EEC and compound fertilisers where the nitrogen content derived from the ammonium nitrate exceeds 28% of the mixture by weight	1000
41.	2.2-Bis(tert-butylperoxy)butane (>70%)	5
42.	1.1-Bis(tert-butylperoxy)cyclohexane (>80%)	5
43.	tert-Butyl peroxyacetate (>70%)	5
44.	tert-Butyl peroxyisobutyrate (>80%)	5
45.	tert-Butyl peroxyisopropyicarbonate (>80%)	5
46.	tert-Butyl peroxymaleate (>80%)	5
47.	tert-Butyl peroxypivalate (>77%)	5
48.	Cellulose nitrate other than-	
	(i) cellulose nitrate to which the Explosives Act 1875 applies; or (ii) solutions of cellulose nitrate where the nitrogen content of the cellulose nitrate does not exceed 12.3% by weight and the solution contains not more than 55 parts of cellulose nitrate per 100 parts by weight of solution	50
49.	Dibenzyl peroxydicarbonate (>90%)	5
50.	Diethyl peroxydicarbonate (>30%)	5
51.	2.2-Dihydroperoxypropane (>30%)	5
52.	Di-isobutryl peroxide (>50%)	5
53.	Di-n-propyl peroxydicarbonate (>80%)	5
54.	Di-sec-butyl peroxydicarbonate (>80%)	5
55.	Ethylene oxide	5
56.	Ethyl nitrate	50

Column 1 Hazardous substances		Column 2 Controlled quantities
		(in *tonnes*, unless otherwise stated)
57.	3,3.6,6.9,9-Hexamethyl-1,2,4, 5-tetroxacyclononane (>75%)	5
58.	Hydrogen	2
59.	Liquid Oxygen	500
60.	Methyl ethyl ketone peroxide (>60%)	5
61.	Methyl isobutyl ketone peroxide (>60%)	5
62.	Peracetic acid (>60%)	5
63.	Propylene oxide	5
64.	Sodium chlorate	25
65.	Sulphur dichloride	1

Part C: Flammable Substances (unless specifically named in Parts A and B)

Column 1 Hazardous substances		Column 2 Controlled quantities
		(in *tonnes*, unless otherwise stated)
66.	Liquefied petroleum gas, such as commercial propane and commercial butane, and any mixtures thereof, when held at a pressure greater than 1.4 bar absolute	25

Column 1 Hazardous substances		Column 2 Controlled quantities
		(in *tonnes*, unless otherwise stated)
67.	Liquefied petroleum gas, such as commercial propane and commercial butane, and any mixture thereof, when held under refrigeration at a pressure of 1.4 bar absolute or less	50
68.	Gas or any mixture of gases which is flammable in air, when held as a gas	15
69.	A substance or any mixture of substances, which is flammable in air, when held above its boiling point (measured at 1 bar absolute) as a liquid or as a mixture of liquid and gas at a pressure of more than 1.4 bar absolute	25
70.	A liquefied gas or any mixture of liquefied gases, which is flammable in air and has a boiling point of less than 0°C (measured at 1 bar absolute), when held under refrigeration or cooling at a pressure of 1.4 bar absolute or less	50
71.	A liquid or any mixture of liquids not included in entries 68 to 70 above, which has a flash point of less than 21°C	10,000

Part D: Interpretation

In this Schedule:

(a) references to percentages are references to parts by weight of the substance per 100 parts by weight of the solution;

(b) "compound fertiliser" means a fertiliser containing ammonium nitrate and phosphate or potash;

(c) Part C does not include a substance which is within Part A or Part B;

(d) a substance, or any mixture or substances, shall only be treated as a hazardous substance by virtue of satisfying a description in entry number 37, 66, 67, 69 or 70 when it is in a state in which it satisfies the description;

(e) the controlled quantity of 25 tonnes in entry 69 refers, in the case of a mixture of substances, to the quantity of substances within that mixture held above their boiling point (measured at 1 bar absolute);

(f) the controlled quantity of 50 tonnes in entry 70 refers, in the case of a mixture of substances, to the quantity of substances within that mixture having boiling points below 0°C

Appendix 4

Useful Addresses, Contacts and Telephone Numbers

HMIP Addresses			
Headquarters	**North Division**	**East Division**	**West Division**
Romney House 43 Marsham Street LONDON SW1P 3PY Tel: 0171 276 8061 Fax: 0171 276 8605	Stockdale House 8 Victoria Road Headingley LEEDS LS6 1PF Tel: 0113 2786636 Fax: 0113 2740464	Howard House 40-64 St John's St BEDFORD MK42 0DL Tel: 01234 272112 Fax: 01234 218355	Highwood Pavilions Jupiter Road Patchway BRISTOL BS12 5SN Tel: 0117 9794653 Fax: 0117 9794650
Health and Safety Commission			
Headquarters	**North West Region**		
Baynards House 1 Chepstow Place Westbourne Grove London W2 4TP Tel: 0171 717 6000 Fax: 0171 727 2254	Magdalen House Stanley Precinct Bootle Merseyside L20 3QZ Tel: 0151 951 4000 Fax 0151 922 5394		
Health and Safety Executive Area Offices			
South West	**South**	**South East**	
Inter City House Mitchell Lane, Victoria Street Bristol BS1 6AN Tel: 0117 9290681	Priestley House Priestley Road Basingstoke RG24 9NW Tel: 01256 473181	3 East Grinstead Hse London Road East Grinstead West Sussex RH19 1RR Tel: 01342 326922	

London North	London South	East Anglia	
Maritime House 1 Linton Road Barking Essex 1G11 8HF Tel: 0181 594 5522	(all construction in London covered by this office) 1 Long Lane London SE1 4PG Tel: 0171 407 8911	39 Baddow Road Chelmsford Essex CM2 0HL Tel: 01245 284661	
Northern Home Counties	**East Midlands**	**West Midlands**	**Wales**
14 Cardiff Road Luton Beds LU1 1PP Tel: 01582 34121	Belgrave House 1Greyfriars Northampton NN1 2BS Tel: 01604 21233	McLaren Building 2 Masshouse Circus Queensway Birmingham B4 7NP Tel: 0121 200 2299	Brunel House Fitzalan Road Cardiff CF2 1SH
HSE Information Centres	**Marches**	**North Midlands**	**South Yorkshire and Humberside**
Broad Lane Sheffield S3 7HQ Tel: 0114 2752539 Fax: 0114 2720006	The Marches House Midway Newcastle Upon Tyne Staffs ST5 1DT Tel: 0178 2717181	Birbeck House Trinity Square Nottingham NG1 4AU Tel: 0115 9470712	Sovereign House 40 Silver Street Sheffield S1 2ES Tel: 0114 2739081
West and North Yorkshire	**Greater Manchester**	**Merseyside**	**North West**
8 St Paul's Street Leeds LS1 2LE Tel: 0113 2446191	Quay House Quay Street Manchester M3 3JB Tel: 0161 831 7111	The Triad Stanley Road Bootle L20 3PG Tel: 0151 922 7211	Victoria House Ormskirk Road Preston PR1 1HH Tel: 01772 59321
North East	**Scotland East**	**Scotland West**	
Arden House Regent Centre Gosforth Newcastle Upon Tyne NE3 3JN Tel: 0191 284 8448	Belford House 59 Belford Road Edinburgh EH4 3UE Tel: 0131 225 1313	314 St Vincent St Glasgow G3 8XG Tel: 0141 204 2646	

NRA OFFICES			
Head Office – London	**Head Office – Bristol**	**Northumbria & Yorkshire Region**	**North West Region**
30-34 Albert Embankment London SE1 7TL Tel: 0171 820 0101	Rivers House Waterside Drive Aztec West Almondsbury Bristol BS12 4UD Tel: 0117 9624400	Rivers House 21 Park Square South Leeds LS1 2DG Tel: 0113 2440191	Richard Fairclough House Knutsford Road Warrington WA4 1HG Tel: 0192 553999
Welsh Region	**Severn-Trent Region**	**Anglian Region**	**Thames Region**
Rivers House Plas-yr-Afon St Mellons Business Park St Mellons Cardiff CF3 0LT Tel: 01222 770088	Sapphire East Streetsbrook Road Solihull West Midlands B91 1QT Tel: 0121 7112324	Kingfisher House Goldhay Way Orton Goldhay Peterborough PE2 0ZR Tel: 01733 371811	Kings Meadow House Kings Meadow Road Reading RG1 8DQ Tel: 01734 535000
Southern Region Guildbourne House Chatsworth Road Worthing West Sussex BN11 11D Tel: 01903 820692	**South West & Wessex Region** Manley House Kestrel Way Exeter EX2 7LQ Tel: 01392 444000		
Office of Water Services (OFWAT)			
The Director General Centre City Tower 7 Hill Street Birmingham B5 4UA Tel: 0121 625 1300			

Water Company Addresses			
Anglian Water Services Limited Compass House Chivers Way Histon Cambridgeshire CB4 4ZY Tel: 01223 372000 Fax: 01223 372271	**Northumbrian Water Limited** Abbey Road Pity Me Durham DH1 5FJ Tel: 0191 383 2222 Fax: 0191 384 1920	**North West Water Limited** Dawson House Great Sankey Warrington WA5 3LW Tel: 01925 234000 Fax: 01925 233360	**Severn Trent Water Limited** Abelson House 2297 Coventry Road Sheldon Birmingham B26 3PU Tel: 0121 722 4000 Fax: 0121 722 8400
South West Water Services Limited Peninsula House Rydon Lane Exeter EX2 7RH Tel: 01392 219666 Fax: 01392 434966	**Thames Water Utilities Limited** Negent House Vastern Road Reading RG1 8DB Tel: 01734 591159 Fax: 01723 593203	**Dwr Cymru – Welsh Water** Plas-y-ffynnon Cambrian Way Brecon Powys LD3 7HP Tel: 01874 623181 Fax: 01874 624167	**Wessex Water Services Limited** Wessex House Passage Street Bristol BS2 0JQ Tel: 0117 9290611 Fax: 0117 9293137
Southern Water Services Limited Southern House Yeoman Road Worthing Sussex BN13 3NN Tel: 01903 64444 Fax: 01903 62185	**Yorkshire Water Services Limited** West Riding House 67 Albion Street Leeds LS1 5AA Tel: 0113 2448201 Fax: 0113 2443071	**Bournemouth And West Hampshire Water Company** George Jessel House Francis Avenue Bournemouth BH11 8NB Tel: 01202 572261 Fax: 01202 579059	**Bristol Waterworks Company** P O Box 218 Bridgwater Road Bristol BNS99 7AU Tel: 0117 9665881 Fax: 0117 9633755
Cambridge Water Company Rustat Road Cambridge CB1 3QS Tel: 01223 247351 Fax: 01223 214052	**Chester Waterworks Company** Aqua House 45 Boughton Chester CH3 5AU Tel: 01244 320501 Fax: 01244 316102	**Cholderton and District Water Company** Estate Office Cholderton Salisbury Tel: 0198 064203	**[Colne Valley Water Company]** Now Three Valleys Water Services Plc

[Eastbourne Water] Now South East Water	**East Surrey Water Plc** London Road Redhill Surrey RH1 1LJ Tel: 01737 765933 Fax: 01737 766807	**East Worcestershire Waterworks** 46 New Road Bromsgrove Worcestershire B60 2JT Tel: 01527 75151 Fax: 01527 78203	**Essex Water Company** Hall Street Chelmsford Essex CM2 0HH Tel: 01245 419234 Fax: 01245 491271
Folkstone & District Water Company Cherry Garden Lane Folkstone Kent CT19 4QB Tel: 01303 276951 Fax: 01303 276712	**Hartlepools Water Company** 3 Lancaster Road Hartlepool TS24 8LW Tel: 01429 274405 Fax: 01429 278961	**[Lee Valley Water Company]** Now Three Valleys Water Services Plc	**Mid Kent Water Company** P O Box 45 High Street Scotland Kent ME6 5AH Tel: 01634 240313 Fax 01634 242764
Mid Southern Water Company Frimley Green Camberley Surrey GU16 6HZ Tel: 01252 835031 Fax: 01252 836066	**[Mid-Sussex Water Company]** Now South East Water	**[Newcastle & Gateshead Water Company]** Now North East Water Plc	**North East Water Plc** P O Box 10 Allendale Road Newcastle Upon Tyne NE6 2SW Tel: 0191 2654144 Fax: 0191 2766612 [Newcastle & Gateshead And Sunderland & South Shields Water Companies]
North Surrey Water Company Millis House The Causeway Staines Middlesex TW18 3BX Tel: 017894 455464 Fax: 01764 451260	**Portsmouth Water Plc** P O Box 8 West Street Havant Hants PO9 1LG Tel: 01705 486333 Fax: 01705 453632	**[Rickmansworth Water Company]** Now Three Valleys Water Services Plc	**South East Water** 14 Upperton Road Eastbourne Sussex BN212 1EP Tel: 01323 411411 Fax: 01323 411412 [Eastbourne Mid-Sussex and West Kent Water Companies]

South Staffordshire Waterworks Company Green Lane Walsall West Midlands WS2 7PD Tel: 01922 38282 Fax: 01922 21968	**Suffolk Water Plc** 163 High Street Lowestoft Suffolk NR32 1HT Tel: 01502 572406 Fax: 01502 517039	**[Sunderland & South Shields Water Company]** Now North East Water Plc	**Sutton District Water Plc** 59 Gander Green Lane Cheam Sutton Surrey SM1 2EW Tel: 0181 6438050 Fax: 0181 6344461
Tendering Hundred Waterworks Company Manningtree Essex CO11 2AZ Tel: 01206 392155 Fax: 01206 395541	**Three Valleys Water Services Plc** P O Box 48 Bishop's Rise Hatfield Herts AL10 9HL Tel: 01707 268111 Fax: 01707 276629 [Colne Valley, Lee Valley And Rickmansworth Water Companies]	**[West Hampshire Water Company]** Now Bournemouth And West Hampshire Water Company	**[West Kent Water Company]** Now South East Water
Wrexham & East Denbighshire Water Company 21 Egerton Street Wrexham Clywd L11 1ND Tel: 01978 219777 Fax: 01978 622171	**York Waterworks Plc** Lendal Tower York YO1 2DL Tel: 01904 622171 Fax: 01904 611667		

Central Government contacts for Environmental Issues

Acid Rain Alastair McKay Department of the Environment 0171 276 8165	**Farm Odours** Bronwen Jones Ministry of Agriculture, Fisheries and Food 0171 238 5669
Industrial Air Pollution **Local Authorities** Mike Etkind Department of the Environment 0171 276 8323 Other Jeff Hockley Her Majesty's Inspectorate of Pullution 0171 276 8148	**Biological agents including Legionnaires' Disease** Peter Lister Health & Safety Executive 0171 243 6112
Vehicle Emissions Tony Baker Department of Transport 0171 276 6428 Hannah Saunders Department of the Environment 0171 276 8312 Industrial Interests Josephine Cook Department of Trade and Industry 0171 215 1177	**Volatile organic compounds (VOCs)** Alastair McKay Department of the Environment 0171 276 8165 John Spong Department of Trade and Industry 0171 215 1017
Human Health & Safety Stuart Smith Health & Safety Executive 0171 243 6120 Environment Aspects John Palfaavy Department of the Environment 0171 276 8327 Biotechnology for pollution abatement Peter Nolan Laboratory of the Government Chemist 0181 943 7381 Health-related aspects Dr David Harper Department of Health 0171 972 5353	**Cleaner technology and industrial waste minimisation** Douglas Robinson Department of Trade and Industry 0171 215 1027 John Thompson Department of the Environment 0171 276 8315

Best Practice DTI David Johnson Department of Trade and Industry 0171 215 1065 Ken Nully Department of Trade and Industry 0171 276 8146	**Building Research Establishment (BRE)** Advice on the impacts of buildings and their components on global, local and indoor environments. Roger Baldwin Building Research Establishment 01923 664223
Laboratory of the Government Chemist (LGC) Scientific programmes to monitoring asbestos, contaminated water and land, radionuclide,s pesticide residues and microbiological hazards. Ian Rix Laboratory of the Government Chemist 0181 943 7377	**National Engineering Laboratory (NEL)** Comprehensive engineering technology services and consultancy. In-depth knowledge of renewable energy, process energy efficiency, recycling, waste treatment, machine noise and internal combustion engines, and how they relate to environmental issues. Peter Walker NEL 013552 76081
National Physical Laboratory (NPL) Standards and traceable measurements for air quality; standards gas mixtures; developing and exploiting new techniques for industrial and urban air pollution measurement. Peter Woods National Physical Laboratory 0181 943 7095	**Transport Research Laboratory (TRL)** Roads and transport research UK and overseas; environmental appraisal including vehicle emissions, pollution, noise, spray, ecological effects, social surveys and engineering solutions. Charles Downing Transport Research Laboratory 01344 770004

Warren Spring Laboratory (WSL) Environmental measurement and analysis, investigating techniques for preventing and remedying pollution; waste minimisation and recycling; materials handling and separation technologies. Warren Spring Laboratory will merge with AEA Technology to form The National Environmental Technology Centre on 1 April 1994. Neil Hurford Warren Spring Laboratory 01438 741122 Extn 2246	**Chemical Risk Assessment** Robert Woodward Health & Safety Executive 0171 243 6000 John Rea Department of the Environment 0171 276 8325 Robert Woodward Health & Safety Executive 0171 243 6000 Environment effects John Rea Department of the Environment 0171 276 8156 Teresa Quinn Health & Safety Executive 0171 243 6834
Substitution for banned or restricted chemicals Robert Woodward Health & Safety Executive 0171 243 6000	**Chemical substances labelling** Mike Mahoney Health & Safety Executive 0171 243 6282 Dr Steven Robertson Department of the Environment 0171 276 8913
Controlling environmental claims The Trade Descriptions Act 1968 Karen Hutchinson Department of Trade and Industry 0171 215 3292	**Ecolabelling** Cara Cooper UK Ecolabelling Board 0171 820 1199
Energy Labelling Ray Morgan Department of the Environment 0171 276 4671	**Food Labelling** Sharon Taylor Ministry of Agriculture, Fisheries & Food 0171 238 6463

Ozone Layer Geoff Tierney Department of the Environment 0171 276 8621 Terry Martin Department of Trade and Industry 0171 215 1018	**Contaminated Land** Investigation and assessment of contaminated land – government guidance. Colin Grant Department of the Environment 0171 276 8481 Contamination and treatment – techical issues. Environmental enquiry point Freephone 0800 585 794
Food Chain Protection Colin Mylchreest Ministry of Agriculture, Fisheries & Food 0171 270 8126	**Policy** Sara Sturrick Department of the Environment 0171 276 8140 Steve Adams Department of Trade and Industry 0171 215 1038 Mike Etkind Department of the Environment 0171 276 8482

General Policy advice Brian Fullam Health & Safety Executive 0151 951 3251 (Environment issues only) Bill Parish Department of the Environment 0171 276 8366 **Site Specific advice** Health & Safety Executive Public Enquiry Point 01742 892345	**Noise** Aircraft noise Chris Shoreman Department of Transport 0171 276 5328 **Environmental and neighbourhood noise** Mary Dyer Department of the Environment 0171 276 8482 **Noise Control Industry** Health and Safety Executive Public Enquiry Point 01742 892345 **Railway noise** Nick Dole Department of Transport 0171 276 6651 **Vehicle noise standards** Tony Baker Department of Transport 0171 276 6428 James Marsh Department of Trade and Industry 0171 215 1034 Geoff Lang Department of the Environment 0171 276 8471

Biofuels/passive solar Adam Brown Energy Technology Support Unit 01235 433585 **Wind/tidal/hydro/wave/geothermal** Ray Taylor Energy Technology Support Unit 01235 433601 **General Enquiries** Renewal Energy Enquiries Bureau Energy Technology Support Unit 01235 433601	**Agricultural Waste** Graham Lewis Ministry of Agriculture, Fisheries & Food 0171 238 5689 **Duty of Care** Paul Wright Department of the Environment 0171 276 8462 **Hazardous Waste** Duncan Egerton Department of the Environment 0171 276 8505
Litter Nick Allan Department of the Environment 0171 276 8862	**Waste Disposal** Verity Sherwood Department of the Environment 0171 276 8458 **Local Authority Waste** Disposal Companies Godfrey Souter 0171 276 8270 **Licensing appeal system** Diane Reed Department of the Environment 0171 276 8829 **Waste imports** Richard Longman Department of the Environment 0171 276 8829 **Waste minimisation** Douglas Robinson Department of Trade and Industry 0171 215 1027

Water Quality **Agricultural nitrate pollution** Paul Smith Ministry of Agriculture, Fisheries & Food 0171 238 5715	**EC Directives relating to dangerous** **substances in surface waters** Andree Sheeham-Evett Department of the Environment 0171 276 8276
Analytical methods David Westwood Department of the Environment 0171 276 8298	**Marine Environment** Sean Ryan Department of the Environment 0171 276 8504 Graham Boyes Ministry of Agriculture, Fisheries & Food 0171 238 5868
New Chemicals and materials Howard Rogers Department of the Environment 0171 276 8901	**Private Water Supplies** David Hampson Department of the Environment 0171 276 8845
Quality of inland and tidal waters Kim Logan Department of the Environment 0171 276 8282	**Water Byelaws** Paul Fletcher Department of the Environment 0171 276 8130
Water Research Paul Harry Department of the Environment 0171 276 8696	

Further Sources of Information	British Library	Environmental Helpline
ACBE: The Environment – A Business Guide. Produced by the Department of Trade and Industry on behalf of The Advisory Committee on Business and the Environment (ACBE), this booklet provides an introduction to environmental issues for business and lists key publications and sources of advice. Copies are available from the Director Marketing Centre. 01443 821877	The British Library's Environmental Information Service provides a central access point for British Library resources and is able to answer free quick enquiries, or carry out detailed research on a priced basis. Document supply, online searches, official publications, science & technology literature, patents and business information in the environmental field are available through the service. British Library 0171 323 7955	The Helpline is a Department of Trade and Industry telephone enquiry service producing a comprehensive information and signposting service for firms wishing to find out about environmental pollution issues that may affect their business. Telephone calls are free. 0800 585 794
The United Kingdom Environmental Law Association, 61 Charterhouse Street, London EC1M 6HA (Membership Secretary Malcolm Forster, c/o Freshfields, 65 Fleet Street, London EC4Y 1HS Tel: 0171 936 4000)		
British Geological Survey Keyworth Nottingham NG12 5GG Tel: 01602 363100		**Soil Survey and Land Research Centre** Silsoe Bedford MK45 4DT Tel: 01525 860428

Index